THE LOST BLOGS

THE LOST
BLOGS
FROM JESUS TO JIM MORRISON

The Historically **INACCURATE** and
Totally **FICTITIOUS** Cyber **DIARIES**
of **EVERYONE WORTH KNOWING**

PAUL DAVIDSON

WARNER BOOKS

NEW YORK   BOSTON

Warner Books

Time Warner Book Group
1271 Avenue of the Americas, New York, NY 10020
Visit our Web site at www.twbookmark.com.

Printed in the United States of America

First Edition: May 2006

10 9 8 7 6 5 4 3 2 1

Library of Congress Cataloging-in-Publication Data
Davidson, Paul
    The lost blogs : from Jesus to Jim Morrison : the historically inaccurate and totally fictitious cyber diaries of everyone worth knowing / Paul Davidson. - - 1st ed.
            p. cm.
    "A humorous compilation of blogs 'written' by 175 historical figures and celebrities, showing what really went on inside the greatest minds of all time. " - - Provided by the publisher.
        ISBN-13: 978-0-446-69738-5
        ISBN-10: 0-446-69738-9
    1. Celebrities - - Humor. I. Title.

PN6231.C25D38 2006
818' . 602 - - dc22

2005037193

Book design and text composition by HRoberts Design

Acknowledgments

May the thanking portion of this book begin . . . *now.*

First and foremost I would like to thank my agent, Arielle Eckstut, from the Levine Greenberg Agency. Arielle has been there for me through thick and thin (weeks 1–3 of the South Beach Diet) and has been a supportive, knowledgeable partner in crime. And although we actually never participated in any real *actual* crimes together (except the liberating of a pack of gum from an undisclosed location), I would still rather die than tell anyone our secrets. I'm trained like that. Go ahead and try me. I would also like to thank my editor, Jason Pinter, from Warner Books, for his sense of humor, his knowledge of dead historical people, and his passion for the content herein. Or therein. (If *herein* refers to past tense then use that. If *therein* is the right word, use that instead.) He has been a pleasure to work with and nothing like the evil editors you read about in Page Six. Except, come to think of it, he does have one of those knives holstered just above his left knee, but he says that's for peeling apples and I'm inclined to believe him.

I would like to thank my manager, Chris Emerson. I would like to thank my agent, Craig Kestel, at the William Morris Agency. I would like to thank their assistants. And the companies that flip the switch to allow their cell phones to work, which in turn allows them to talk to me. I would like to thank the guy who invented phones, who happens to be included in this book, and I would like to thank book people in general, for liking books and reading books and using them to prop up rickety old tables that have that wobbly disease going on. (If you use this book for that and I find out I will not be thanking you in the next book.)

I would like to thank the people who had conversations with me that went a little something like this:

ME: *Have you ever heard of Abe Vigoda?*
THEM: *No, who's Abe Vigoda?*
ME: *The guy from that old TV show* Fish *and* Barney Miller.
THEM: *There was a TV show called* Fish? *That's so funny.*
ME: *Yeah, Bea Arthur was in it.*
THEM: *Oh, I don't like Bea Arthur.*
ME: *Fine, but do you think I should include Abe Vigoda in the book?*
THEM: *Who's Abe Vigoda again?*

I would like to thank Brigid Pearson, the talented designer who came up with the cover for the book. I would like to thank the model whose body we used on the cover of the book because he looks as hairy as I suspect Abe Lincoln probably was. I would like to thank the photographer who took the picture of the Abe Lincoln model for doing such a great lighting job and making it look as tasteful as it does.

I would also like to thank Jeff and Mark Grammatke, Fabian Marquez, Brian Rousso, Kevin Kelly, Kristine Howard, Meagan Montisci, Bob Castillo, Anna Maria Piluso, Elly Weisenberg, Daniel Greenberg, Mark Cuban, and all the frequent and not-so-frequent readers of *Words for My Enjoyment* for their continued enthusiasm, support, and commentary. I would have thanked the guy to whom I had to send a ham after awarding it as a prize for one of those online contests, but that ham cost over fifty bucks so that's all the thanks he needs.

Finally, I would like to thank the family. Without thanking the family, I'm just the bastard who didn't thank the family instead of the guy who thanked the family and wrote a really funny book—so I should go ahead and thank them now: Thanks to Mom and Dad for their support and almost unhealthy blind approval. Thanks to Sari, Matt, Jake, Bonnie, Harold, John, and Briel. Thanks must also go out to the guy at the coffee shop who knows what I like to drink (and sometimes gives me two card punches when no one is looking) and, therefore, should be categorized as family as well.

Finally, thanks must be heaped upon the one they call *Jennifer*. Normally, if you lived in a house with someone (me) who had spontaneous mood swings, talked in tongues, and often laughed out loud about practically nothing all the time, you would call yourself a therapist, psychiatrist, or medical technician. Jennifer, it seems, likes to go by the title *wife*. It seems that her loss is wholly my gain—and I love her for it.

[Insert end of thank you page theme music here. The one with the horns and harpsichord.]

THE LOST BLOGS

From: **http://www.moses.com/blog/**

Subject: **A Pretty Astounding Day**

My previous entries concerning the burning bush and the locusts that descended upon Egypt can be read <u>here</u> and <u>here</u>. The reason behind mentioning such writings now is only so that you may fully grasp the majesty that is the Lord in the next story I wish to share with all of you.

Please bear with me, children, as I am sending this entry from my holy portable communication device—so punctuation and proper grammar may fail me. May the Lord forgive any of my shortcomings.

The <u>Free the Slaves of Egypt Webring</u>, which continues to function as I communicate with you today, has previously mentioned the plight of the Jewish people. You have read about <u>the ten plagues</u> and yesterday's <u>mass exodus out of Egypt</u>. Today I moblog to you from the other side of the Red Sea.

Yes, my children—you heard correctly. The **other side** of the Red Sea.

I stood before God's waters with hundreds of thousands of our people by my side. The Egyptians, as previously mentioned in yesterday's <u>entry</u>, were closing in on us. There was no place to go. We were trapped.

Yet my faith in the Lord transformed the situation from hopeless to hope-filled.

Without warning, God caused the waters to part for the people of Israel. I took a few pictures with my holy portable communication device, which includes a holy eye that can collect images which can be viewed <u>here</u>. The quality is not the best, but if you just feel one-half of the wonder that I felt—you will understand the feeling that swept the crowd. There's a close-up shot of me <u>here</u> waving at the Egyptians as they drowned in the rapidly filling sea. (You may not be able to fully see this in the pictures, that's why I must mention that once we were all safely across, the waters began to fill back in. It was a glorious moment.)

Now free of our bonds and of the Egyptians, we will make our way to Israel. I may not be posting as often over the next few weeks, as I must conserve my holy communication device's holy life of battery power for the important moments.

If you're looking for something to read while I'm gone, please check out <u>Pharaoh's Blog</u>, which will, I'm quite sure, contain some fairly amusing observations about yesterday's incident involving me and the chosen people of Israel.

From: **http://www.johnwilkesbooth.org/blog/**

Subject: **A Mediocre Actor Am I?**

As most of you well know by now (thanks to the consistent reporting over at the <u>Unofficial John Wilkes Booth Fan Club</u>) I have been acting out of the Arch Street Theatre here in Philadelphia.

The environment has not felt nurturing to say the least.

I am not getting along with William Fredericks, the acting and stage manager here at Arch Street. He has it out for me, along with the rest of the actors here. Forgotten lines and missed cues are common mistakes in the world of acting. Why they must single yours truly out each time a mistake is made is anyone's guess. I am finding myself getting increasingly frustrated with Fredericks—doesn't he know how tough it is being an actor? I suspect they are whispering about me behind my back.

But before I forget—here is my new head shot:

John Wilkes Booth—"Dramatic"

The above head shot showcases my dramatic side, which I use to perform in plays by Shakespeare and the like. I enjoy such dramatic pursuits. Aaah, drama.

Back to Arch Street. I know that all I can do is my best. But the art of theatre is filled with disappointment. But then again, my colleagues should support me. They have it out for me, I suspect. They are, if I must be so bold to say—evil. There are times I look at them that I see red: the red that one associates with the devil. Isn't it strange, I have often wondered, how one cannot spell the word devil without e, v, i, and l.

Something should be done about these unsupportive colleagues of mine.

However, dear readers— I would love your opinion on this second head shot I recently commissioned a photographer to take of me . . .

John Wilkes Booth: "Comedic"

For those comedic roles—this picture showcases the lighthearted side of yours truly. The silly, carefree, happy side.

Weatley's Arch Street Theatre is small potatoes. Do not think that my goal is to stay here and perform alongside malcontents in a jealous rage. Fame, it seems, does not visit this part of the country. Now, Ford's Theatre—that would be a wonderful place to go, with (I suspect) very little drama of the offstage variety. Where anger would step aside in the name of entertainment.

Sometimes I just want to teach them all a lesson.

Nonetheless—in the meantime, please write me with your thoughts on my new investment—the wonderful head shots of which I have previously highlighted. A third version, my "angry" head shot, can be viewed <u>here</u>.

From: **http://www.baberuth.com/blog/**

Subject: **Baseball Ain't About Singing Songs**

If it wasn't for baseball, I'd be in either the penitentiary or the cemetery. If it wasn't for Red Sox owner/prick Harry Frazee and his lack of backbone when it comes to his dame—I probably wouldn't be packing my bag for New York right now . . .

Here's a picture of my <u>ass</u>. I hope you know this is for you, Frazee.

Thanks for all the notes, people. The sentiment is good. Although I woulda taken half the money they pay me right now to continue playing at Fenway, I guess all I'm worth to Frazee is cold hard cash. The kind that can help him get his girl's musical off the ground. Well, she stinks. Can't sing a lick. Worst investment in the history of the world.

I was in a bit of a downer last night when my buddies came by and we made a night of it. About the time they were draggin' my fat ass home, we passed by this garbage dump of a place run by some lady who calls herself <u>Madame X</u>. We figured, what the hell, and walked on in.

She knew about this old Babe as most people in Boston do—and we got to talkin'. About how Frazee and the Sox weren't treating you know who with the respect he deserved. How Harry's stupid decision to let the Babe go was gonna affect those Sox for longer than they'd ever care to remember. Madame X throws up some powder, there's this flash of light and she tells me "it's all done."

"What's all done?" I ask her.

"You'll see," she says.

About that time, the beer was comin' back up my gullet—so my buddies dragged me off the floor and toward the street. Madame X shouts back to remember the number "2004" or "a thousand four" or "don't fall on the floor"—I'm not sure which . . . Although she seemed all worked up about the number for some reason.

Who knows . . . or cares. Now I got a hangover and I gotta pack my shit up.

Baseball—if it doesn't make you a star, it'll kill you eventually.

From: **http://www.blogs.com/neilarmstrong/**
Subject: **One Small Step for Me!**

There's a lot of technical jargon being thrown around in the Apollo 11 capsule right before we touch down on the Moon. Last week's lunar landing was historical, yes, but even more of a technical feat. The small details are what make something like that extremely successful.

Even more exciting, of course, was that moment right as we touched down on that hunka cheese. That moment, right before the hatch door opens and we step down into History. Thanks to Buzz Aldrin's antics, it went a little something like this:

Buzz: *"I'm gonna head on out, Neil. See you out there?"*
Me: *"Uh, why don't you let me step out there first?"*
Buzz: *"No, no no. Don't worry yourself. You just look at the instruments, talk to Mission Control—it's probably cold out there anyway. Let this lowly lunar module pilot take the beating for you, Commander."*
Collins: *"Or, you could stay behind and I'll go check it out for the both of you."*

Obviously, who would be the first man to step foot on the Moon was the debate of the moment. And so, I reached into the back to my rigorous training at NASA and came up with the perfect solution . . . The kind of way we always used to solve disagreements at the Cape . . .

Me: *"Rock, paper, scissors."*
Buzz: *"Rock, paper, scissors?"*
Collins: *"Rock, paper, scissors!"*
Me: *"First to win three, is the first to step on the Moon. Deal?"*
Buzz: *"Rock, paper, scissors?"*
Collins: *"Rock, paper, scissors!"*

Thirty-eight rounds later, you can imagine the outcome. The exact thirty-eight-round play-by-play can be read <u>here</u>, although is there really any need to take a gander at it? I think we all know who the first man on the Moon was.

First Man on the Moon's Rock/Paper/Scissors Tip of the Day: If you use rock every time, you'll eventually win.

From: http://www.john_lennon.co.uk/blog/

Subject: Met a Girl . . .

Was in London this past weekend and had the pleasure of attending the art exhibit of a strange and fascinating woman named Yoko Ono. Or Ocean Child, as she calls herself.

A child, she is not. Her art was poetic, engaging and thought-provoking. When I attempted to compliment her on the exhibit, she seemed to have no idea who I was. It was, in a world of unwanted attention, quite pleasant.

We talked for some time, of course. I asked about her performance art, she asked me how long I expected to be with the Beatles. I asked about her inspirations and motivations behind some of the pieces on display, and she seemed awfully interested in how Paul and I dealt with the publishing rights of our songs. We talked for what seemed like hours about music, the planet, nature and how long I thought I might stay on with the Beatles before trying solo projects.

She was, to say the least, quite supportive of my singular musical passions—she even encouraged me to explore areas of music I had never thought to attempt before. Areas of music, she said, that only involved one person instead of two, three or four additional performers.

I'm not quite sure where it all will lead, but by the end of the evening we made plans to see each other under a much less formal situation. Much more casual. I suggested possibly attending a play or sharing a table at a restaurant—she suggested possibly taking a trip to an undisclosed location and locking ourselves away for days on end without anyone knowing our whereabouts. Especially the Beatles, she joked. We could strip them of all that makes them who they are, she laughed . . .

A bird with a sense of humor! Absolutely adorable!

From: **http://www.napoleon.fr/blog/**

Subject: **Today's Thoughts on Size**

In my travels across many great continents, I have often come in contact with extremely small men. Midget men so small that they often find themselves misplaced under foot and hoof. Tiny little small men that measure barely three feet or four feet tall. I feel sorry for such men, if you could even call them men—I wouldn't personally call them men, as they are so short. In fact, short isn't really an appropriate word for such maladies. A man is not a man if he is less than five feet tall. Of this I am sure. For if you are not tall enough to look into the eyes of another man, you are not a full man but instead a small man, which isn't the same as being a full man.

My belief is that if you are less than five feet tall, then yes, you are not fully a man. But if you are over five feet, well, then you are a man and there is no question about such things. And if you are five feet three inches or five feet four inches you are obviously a superior man. If your height reaches above five feet five or five feet six, it is obvious that you are one to be feared. Such height instills fear in your enemies and makes one a superior leader for being able to see farther, higher and deeper.

I have known very few men who measure less than five feet who've won battles or defended their honor. But men above five feet six and three-quarters inches, well, these men are the true official defenders of their countries. Men taller than such measurements cannot be measured by normal human everyday means. Such men are above normal men in both stature and respect.

Again, I will reiterate that I have no concerns of my personal height or measurements (which happens to be five feet seven inches)—this entry is only to express my general thoughts on size. I have picked random numbers and hypothetical measurements, of course, in an attempt to educate and inform. But I am sure that after reading my previous thoughts on size (<u>Entries 1–75</u>, <u>Entries 110–54</u>, <u>Supplemental Entries 198–255</u>, <u>Once Deleted and Now Restored Subentries 422–87</u>), you will see that I am fully unbiased and am simply exploring such subject matter in an attempt to educate and inform those who have previously wondered if size does matter.

I originally had a picture of myself towering over a building, but this has since been taken down due to my desire to not point undue attention toward my stature and how it towers over huge hulking publicly erected buildings. I also removed a photo of me standing next to my soldiers, reaching high into the sky while these tiny dwarfs stood beside me, also to not single my superior self out from the group as a whole. I am many things, but not one who seeks attention.

On an unrelated note, I am seeking a new saddle for my horse—one that supports the weight and height of a five foot seven inch individual, as my current saddle cannot support my five foot seven inch height. <u>E-mail</u> me.

From: **http://www.jamesdean.com/**

Welcome to the Official
James Dean Website

ABOUT | EMAIL ME | MY BELOVED PORSCHE | TIPS ON DRIVING
PICTURES FROM MY LATEST PARTIES | FAVORITE DRINK LIST
WHY SMOKING IS COOL | MY TWENTY-FIVE YEAR CAREER PLAN
AGENTS | MANAGER | ALANON

From: **http://www.billyshakespeare.org/blog/**
Subject: **Art Thou a Critic?**

Having finished my latest opus entitled *Romeo and Juliet* (which you can read <u>here</u>, or watch unfold in moving <u>ASCII animation</u>), and finding pleasure in the creation of such, I was perplex'd upon receiving a note from her Majesty the Queen a fortnight ago. Her opinion (which is highly regarded, if not due to the fact that her fortunes helped assist my literary creations) seems to be that star-crossed lovers Romeo and Juliet should never have left their earthly bodies behind.

"It's depressing," the Queen said. *"Death is saddening and depressing and has no part in a public forum."* Death be not sad? Death hath no place alongside depression? Death is sad. It is depressing. It is public. Nevertheless, the Queen continued . . .

Whilest her suggestion to bring back my beloved Capulet and Montague from wherest forth they rest causes my blood to boil—however, if I ever want to work in this kingdom again, I must prepare myself creatively for compromises of the word. And so, without further adieu I give you the second chapters in the continuing tragedy of my beloved characters . . .

Romeo and Juliet Are Alive!
A fortnight after the deaths of Romeo and Juliet, the kingdom is overcome with sadness. Their bodies, frail, lay side by side when a mysteriously shrouded figure sprinkles magic upon their lifeless souls. Their bodies dance, their eyes open wide, and the Capulet and Montague have returned, both alive! Yet now, they hunger for human flesh and traipse through the countryside like confused, lumbering fools! They are quick to bring destruction upon both their houses, but in a funny way. Comedy, dear Queen, ensues.

Romeo and Juliet: Curtain Call,
With the night muffled, and day's light peeking through the clouds—a shrouded Romeo and Juliet awaken. Those who surround, surprised at a development such as this. For how could two star-crossed lovers who fell ill from drinking poison—how would life breathe anew into their lungs? A hidden joke, cry the lovers! Soon, all who surround are let in on the drama that has been perpetrated upon them as a curtain reveals the audience. Everything, including their deaths, acted out for others' amusement! The lovers surprise their audience again by revealing they are not who they seem! Romeo as Juliet, and Juliet as Romeo—they exchange their clothing for the ultimate reveal!

Romeo and Juliet Are Ghosts!
Having tragically lost their lives and looking for revenge, Romeo and Juliet are ghosts who haunt the Capulet and Montague estates, mysteriously forcing heavy jeweled objects onto the floor and causing terror throughout. Such terror, causing the deaths and suicides of both entire families, will be watched by the all-seeing eyes of Romeo and Juliet, who will giggle with laughter as revenge has finally befallen those who forced their own hand. Family comedy/inspirational drama.

I also find my thoughts turning toward a comedy about two princes who misplace their horse and carriage and spend the entire comedy attempting to relocate it, but this is (as I have said) a very rough idea.

From: http://www.jimmorrison.com/blog.html

Subject: New Words for the Doors

Been workin' on a new song tentatively called "Light the Fire" that was inspired by a moment where I had to, um, light a fire. Would love to hear from the fans before we put poetry to paper. Still working out the kinks, so to speak. Communicate at jmorrison@doors.com. Grooooovy!

In the meantime, while you're doing that . . . check me out—I'm naked on the Doors unofficial 24-Hour Webcam.

--

Light the Fire

You know I've opened up the flume,
And thrown inside a rubber tire
So can you please just follow through?
And finally, please, just start the fire?

Come on baby, light the fire
Come on baby, light the fire
But please don't light the house on fire

The time to hesitate is through
You may as well follow me, your Sire
Pick up a match before I snooze
Falling asleep to the Vienna Boys Choir

Come on baby, light the fire
Come on baby, light the fire
But please don't light the house on fire

The logs and newspapers are new
That smell will be the burning tire

I'll slip off all my clothes and shoes
If you'll just start to light this fire

Come on baby, light the fire
Come on baby, light the fire
It appears as if you've lit the house on fire

You know that I will probably sue
You know that I'll call you a liar
All I'll say is, "Baby, shoo"
This damage is all from your damn fire

Come on baby, light the fire
Come on baby, light the fire
Yes, you started one big fire
Yes, you started one big fire
Yes, the situation's dire
Yes, you started one big fire

Really, I'm feeling it. Poetic, isn't it? Thoughts are welcome!

From: **http://www.jacksonpollock.org/~blog/**

Subject: **No Milk**

I woke up this morning and I quickly ran downstairs because I was thirsty and when I'm thirsty you know I've gotta have something to drink so did I mention I ran downstairs, not really running but sort of walking with a skip which is a half run, but kind of a walk and I got myself down to the kitchen where my wife Lee was already sitting at the kitchen table eating some toast which I by the way am really a fan of and also drinking a great big glass of milk. Well, you can imagine when I asked Lee where the rest of the milk was she just looked at me with this look on her face, the kind of look that the cat who has just eaten the mouse or some big piece of food that fell on the floor below the kitchen table (which has happened before believe it or not) because Lee had accidentally but on purpose finished all of the milk without thinking that I would like to come downstairs after a late night of painting and have a drink of milk myself well you can imagine her response to me turning the kitchen table on its back and causing the milk and the flowers and her books to fall all over the place and to tell you the truth I was glad that I did it because if I can't have milk then she can't have milk and it sort of ends up being an equal situation for two people like us who are out of milk.

I think I just heard Lee get in the car to go get more milk.

Just what kind of milk she's going to get well I told her the kind that she should get and while she was at it I suggested her possibly getting a loaf of bread because what we have sitting on our kitchen counter is at least two weeks old and it's just not that often that we leave the property to fill the kitchen with the items that we so desperately need yet I find it ironic that although we need such items desperately that we instead choose to starve ourselves and fill our bellies with the likes of vodka and rum and scotch instead which I'm not fully complaining about but which I find ironic as I previous mentioned.

I'm feeling a tad tired today mixed with a little bit of fatigue which really I can't quite figure out why a feeling like that is overwhelming me …

Sure it may have something to do with being up all night working on my latest painting which if you're curious which some of you have been which has come my way as a result of many e-mails all asking what I'm working on well let me tell you that this latest piece has red and black and blue and white and orange and a gray color and some white/black areas and something that looks a little bit like a banana after it's been sitting on a street for a few days and a bunch of other mixtures of the previous colors into splashes and stripes and little dots and some bigger dots and some halfway in the middle dots which is the kind of dots that most painters don't employ 'cause who wants to use a medium dot when you can go really small or really huge and a collection of other colors which I don't want to reveal at the moment for fear of giving away exactly what it looks like.

More later, when I have more energy.

From: **http://www.alexanderthegreat.com**

Subject: **The Greatest Blog in the History of Blogs!**

This is the greatest blog ever.

I have seen other blogs and I must be honest in telling you all that this blog would crush all other blogs if they were given weapons and set against each other in a blog-like coliseum of sorts. In fact, if this blog was unarmed and was put face-to-face in a battle with other blogs that were all given some kind of heavy weapon, this blog would still destroy all other blogs.

That's a pretty great blog (one that can destroy other armed blogs with its bare hands) if you ask me which you probably are asking at this very moment, which is why I've answered. Because had I not answered, well, this blog would not be as great as we all know it is.

It's not that I have any ill will to heap upon other blogs . . .

No, yes I do.

I loathe all other blogs because they cannot ascend to the greatness that the great Alexander the Great Official Blog has reached. They may only wish to become a great blog as this one has become, and let good enough alone. This blog is the ultimate of all blogs and any blog that challenges this blog will find their text destroyed in a pile of . . . text. Er, or bloody something . . . in a blog kind of way.

As this blog is the greatest blog in the world, I have established a variety of other great services for you, the great readers of the greatest blog in the world. They include (links are below):

The Greatest Blog's Greatest Forum in the World
The Greatest Blog's Greatest Picture Gallery in the World
The Greatest Blog's Greatest Links in the World
The Greatest Blog's Greatest Background Theme Music in the World
The Greatest Blog's Greatest Classic Posts About Being So Great
Pictures of Me, Alexander the Great
A Link to the Greatest E-mail Address in the World

Thank you, again, for visiting the greatest blog in the world. (Although, really, I shouldn't be thanking you, but you should be thanking me for the great experience you are currently taking part in.)

One last note: To ehrudt@romanempire.com who wrote, *"Your blogeth sucketh, all you do is talk about yourselfeth!"* I would like to officially declare war on ehrudt's family and household, which I will destroy upon finding out just where ehrudt lives.

From: **http://www.blogs.com/rodserling/**
Subject: **Nightmare at 20,000 Feet**

It's been some time since I've written here on the blog, as I've been inundated with *Requiem for a Heavyweight*, which you've all sent wonderful e-mails to me about. Thank you for the kind words, it was an amazing experience as you can very well imagine.

But I didn't plan on using this space to talk about working with Jack Palance or the problematic nature of live TV. Instead, something curious happened to me on my flight back home, of which I'd like to share.

I was sitting in the business class section of the airplane, wedged in between a nice old woman and a window. It was, unfortunately, a stormy night, and the plane was being pushed and pulled in a variety of directions. My neighbor, a woman of about sixty-five, was none too pleased with the turbulence but found her salvation in a pair of very strong drinks which quickly removed the worry from her face. Soon after, she was three sheets to the wind and off in her own world of slumber.

As for me, sitting in the darkness of the cabin, my eyes turned toward the window next to me. Looking out into the night sky on such a rainy night, there was little to see. It struck me deep inside, the idea that anything could be out there. And then, it happened . . .

"That will be one-fifty," a woman's voice said.

I turned, and you can imagine my surprise when I saw the stewardess, with her outstretched palm, asking for money.

"But I didn't order a drink," I told her.

"It was right there," she demanded. *"I saw it right there on your tray."*

Yet there was no drink there. I had not seen a drink. A bottle. Nothing. Yet she insisted she had seen it with such determination, it was scary.

"I saw nothing," I told her. *"And I didn't order a thing."*

Then my neighbor was awakened by the discussion and she, too, weighed in on the situation. She chimed in that she had seen it as well. Before long, it became an eerie conversation about whether I had seen it, if it had mysteriously appeared then disappeared, and whether I was insane. The stewardess, on the other hand, was getting extremely volatile.

"So, you're telling me I'm crazy," she ranted. *"That I'm seeing things?"*

"No, not crazy," I told her. *"Maybe just a little bit fatigued? Overworked?"*

You could see the beads of sweat rolling down her face as she struggled with the thought.

After another fifteen minutes of arguing and a few additional stewardesses joining in on the mystery of the phantom vodka bottle, I gave in and paid the money. My sleep was worth much more than such a strange and eerie argument.

And as I drifted off to sleep, 20,000 feet above the ground, I turned my mind to what my next writing or producing project might be. But honestly, the events that had just transpired had sucked the creative juices out of me. My mind was a blank . . .

When I get back home, maybe then an idea will hit me.

From: **http://www.jimmyKblog.com/***

Subject: **The Latest**

I believe it has been some time since I've updated my blog. As you can imagine, things have been awfully busy down at my job where I have been working extremely long and arduous hours.

I have, however, continued to receive a wide array of e-mails from a wide array of attractive young women who have been so kind to have included high-glossy pictures of themselves in their native locales. To answer all your questions—no, I cannot answer each and every one of your letters and so instead I would like to direct you to my FallinLove.com Profile. For those who do not have access to FallinLove.com, you can read my personal profile below (although I strongly encourage all you ladies to sign up for FallinLove.com so we may exchange confidential correspondence):

"I am a dedicated man with strong beliefs, but not so strong that we can't become close friends. I like long walks in the rain, or along the beach, as long as it's just you and me. I'm not into sharing and I especially don't like to be the third wheel—if we're going to hang out it's got to be just you and me. Confidentially, I don't like cameras or digital photography but I do like pictures of you. You're beautiful. You love being with a man like me, who can crush large countries at will—at least, metaphorically it feels that way. Although I love to travel, I would never ever willingly go to places like Russia or Cuba. I believe in true democracy and honesty, as long as it won't get anyone in trouble. I enjoy pets, children and believe in commitment, although I may not be currently ready to settle down. Above all, you want to be with me no matter what time it may be (like, in the middle of the night) or where it might be (like, in a flea bag of a motel . . . haha)—it's about spending time with each other, no matter the laws that I enforce. My job is important, of course, but not more important than spending time with you. E-mail jimmykane@FallinLove.com if you're interested."

Please, continue to send your pictures if you're interested in being with a guy whose influence cannot be matched in all of the free world and who would gladly rescue you from a sinking U-boat (figuratively, of course)! Okay, that was just a line, but you know what I mean.

Sorry about not having any pictures available of myself just yet—still trying to figure out how to upload to the site. Computers can be so *confusing*!

Best-
JimmyK!

*JFK's anonymous blog.

From: **http://www.washington.com/~george/**

Subject: **My Birthday!**

Of all the presents I could have possibly hoped for, my father and mother were nice enough to have given me just what I have been dreaming of.

An axe. A brand-new, shiny axe.

Well, of course I am quite sure you would have done the very same thing I did, had your mother and father presented you with a brand-new axe. That being, of course, to sharpen the edge and prepare one's self for a test of the hardware. And I did just that.

After sharpening the axe back in the stable, I hiked up behind the farm where I found myself face-to-face with one of the larger fruit trees on my family's plantation. It was quite large, yet so was the blade of the axe . . . You can imagine my excitement as I let my strength transfer to the axe's blade.

I chopped and I chopped and I chopped. Quite stunned, I was, watching just how little the axe affected the trunk of the tree. But I labored on, eventually reaching the halfway mark and causing the huge fruit tree to waver. A few more hits and the tree made a deafening sound as it crashed to the ground.

My father was none too pleased as he rushed alongside me, surveying the damage.

Yet my father is a good soul—one with a knowledge of many things, and he turned to me, looking at my hands (which still grasped the axe) and down at the tree and back up at my eyes, and told me that the tree which had fallen at my hands was now close to death. And the fruits it bared, cherries to be exact, would have to be used immediately. "*In a pie,*" said my father. "*And you will have to help eat them.*"

Well, my father was not aware but I had just been served an enormous meal mere hours prior, and my belly was filled to the brim.

Having just chopped down my beloved father's cherry tree in a selfish act of self-satisfaction, I was saddened but still unable to heed his request and so I turned to my father and said to him, "*Father, **I cannot eat a pie.***"

His brow turned downward in the way it usually turned when he was none too please[d] thoughtless actions. He reminded me that since I had caused the tree to fall, I would have to h[elp] in consuming the fruits of my labor.

I told him again, that I could not eat a pie, yet he did not want to listen.

You can imagine, four pies and five hours later that day, the state in which my belly was in. Father attempted to make me feel better amidst my pain, telling me that someday the lesson I had learned would be remembered with such clarity that children far and wide would never eat before chopping down a fruit tree. "*I cannot eat a pie*" would go down in history alongside my name as a cautionary tale to axe-wielding not-so-hungry children everywhere.

And . . . Father *is* always right.

From: **http://www.thecarpentryblog.com/~jesus/**

Subject: **This Week's Projects!**

This week's projects and tips come from <u>Joseph's Carpentry Circus</u> and <u>The Carpenters Circle</u>, not to mention the pleasant people over at <u>The Carpentry Webring</u>. Pictures and step-by-step instructions are available by clicking on the link for each project. Supplies and tools can be purchased many places, but can be found in Nazareth, which is where I always buy my tools.

<u>Building a Bird House</u>
<u>How to Use a Chisel</u>
<u>Hanging a Door in 10 Easy Steps</u>
<u>Building a House, with Just a Few Helping Hands</u>
<u>Wooden Benches for Two</u>
<u>5 Uses for Old Sawdust</u>
<u>Summer Tables for Summer Meals</u>
<u>Foot Stool, Book Rack or Leg Rest</u>

There's also a personal project I've currently been working on—with limited tools (just two pieces of wood, some nails and a chisel). I can show you how to build your own <u>water or wine rack</u> for proud display in your home or workplace.

Any thoughts on this project would be fully appreciated, as it's just a little something I've started to work on, and am currently not sure how many people will find such an item useful, although I found myself wishing the other day that I could have access to both water and wine at the same time without having to go to the cupboard, retrieve wine, then realize after I sat back down on my <u>wooden bench for two</u> that I wanted water and having to get up again to retrieve that.

With my <u>water or wine rack</u> you can store both satisfying thirst-quenchers in one place and never find yourself deficient of either. For what would one do if they only had water but wanted wine? Nothing! You'd be stuck without a solution! This is just why this project is so useful.

Next week, my Carpentry Weblog will have even more in store for all of you "wooden heads" looking for the next great project. Remember, any questions can be sent to <u>JC@carpentryweblog.com</u>. Your e-mails always bless my inbox and I am more than happy to help you in any projects you may currently be undertaking.

From: **http://www.orsonwelles.com/blog/**

Subject: **Citizen Kane's Release**

No thanks to an UNDISCLOSED certain someone who has offered RKO approximately $800,000 to destroy all the prints of my upcoming film, *Citizen Kane* (cough, WILLIAM RANDOLPH HEARST, cough), things have been awfully chaotic as of late.

This ANONYMOUS media giant (ahem, WILLIAM RANDOLPH HEARST, ahem) seems to think that the movie *Citizen Kane* has something to do with his ANONYMOUS and SECRETIVE life, not to mention the life of his ANONYMOUS SIGNIFICANT OTHER (snort, MARION DAVIES, snort), which is categorically, totally untrue.

If you must know, the character of Charles Foster Kane has nothing to do with any overblown newspaper tycoon or idiotic wannabe movie producer nor is it based on any mediocre or talentless Hollywood hack, singer or actress alike. No, *Citizen Kane* is not based on any of these horrible, soulless, hermitlike individuals. Believe it or not, *Citizen Kane* is based on someone named . . . well, why don't we just call this person BILLY ROLPH AMHEARST.

Who is Billy R. Amhearst? Is he a newspaperman? No, although he loves to read a good paper. Does he live inside a huge mansion? No, although he sure loves to drive past them. Has he found love with a starlet of the stage and screen? No, although he loves to go to the movies. *Citizen Kane* is based on this everyday common man named Billy Amhearst and such ANONYMOUS individuals should see fit to end their crusade against RKO Pictures and the individual known as Orson Welles.

Posted by O. Welles on April 22, 1941, at 03:11 AM | Permalink | Comments (5)

COMMENTS

You're such a liar. There's no such person as Billy Rolph Amhearst!!

Posted by: Anonymous | April 22, 1941, 3:15 AM

There is SO such a person as Billy Rolph Amhearst. Idiot. Why don't you at least put your name down there in the comment section, Mr. Hearst!?

Posted by: O. Welles | April 22, 1941, 3:17 AM

I'm not William Hearst. I just think you should admit that there is no such person as Billy Rolph Amhearst and that your entire movie is based on the real William Hearst! Admit it, you talentless hack!

Posted by: J. Smith | April 22, 1941, 3:19 AM

J. Smith!? That's the best name you could come up with, Mr. Hearst?

Posted by: O. Welles | April 22, 1941, 3:21 AM

Go suck an egg, Welles!

Posted by: James Smith II | April 22, 1941, 3:23 AM

From: **http://www.waltdisney.com/blog/**

Subject: **The Next Step**

The secretive news that I've been holding off from sharing with all of you, of course, can now be made public and I wanted to take this opportunity to let all the Disney fans know here on my blog first!

Having purchased over 27,000 acres of land just west of Orlando in Florida, my brother Roy and I are officially announcing plans for what we're calling "The Amazing WalteRoy Disney Parkworld Amusement Town for Kids!" (We're pretty sure this name rolls off the tongue easily.) Many of you have e-mailed asking just how different it will be from Disneyland itself (other than the name), but all I can say at this point is that there's a "world of possibilities" and if you know Disney you'll already have a pretty good idea about what amazing things the future holds . . .

On a totally unrelated note, while in Florida searching out the land that will eventually be the site of "The Amazing WalteRoy Disney Parkworld Amusement Town for Kids!," you can imagine that it was awfully humid and hot there. The weather in Florida is always in the extremes, and the minute you walk outside you find that your entire body sucks up the humidity and it's quite an uncomfortable situation. Let's just say, Southern California has the best weather around!

Nonetheless, I thought I'd share a solution for those planning on visiting Florida in the future—I like to call it, "sticking your head in the freezer." Surprisingly, I was lucky enough to be handed a hotel suite where the air-conditioning did not work and so I had to resort to opening the freezer, sticking my head inside, and leaving it there for some time until my body temperature cooled. And before long, I must tell you—my head was very happy with the low temperatures!

Of course, you can't live your whole day with your head in a freezer, but in between surveys and meetings with local architects and planners, you can imagine I had my head in that freezer keeping myself calm, collected and definitely cool.

Honestly, I felt the most comfortable I had felt during my entire time in Florida while my head was in the freezer. It just goes to show you, you can never be too cool!

Now back in Southern California, we're just finishing production on *The Monkey's Uncle,* which is a hilarious movie that you'll rush to see when it hits theaters next year. It involves a monkey . . . and an uncle! So mark your calendars now, kids!

As usual, if you have any questions you can feel free to <u>e-mail me</u> and I'll try to get back to you as soon as I can!

From: **http://www.george_orwell.co.uk/blog/**
Subject: **Today's Conversation with My Dog**

Sometimes, my dog is more verbose than normal:

Me: *"Hello."*
My Dog: *"Why, hello George."*
Me: *"Well, aren't you in a good mood today."*
My Dog: *"Why, yes George. I am."*
Me: *"Any particular reason why?"*
My Dog: *"Well, I've decided to run for Prime Minister of England."*
Me: *"Is that so."*
My Dog: *"Why yes, it is."*
Me: *"Well let me be the first person to congratulate you for the thought."*
My Dog: *"Well now you're just being condescending."*
Me: *"How so?"*
My Dog: *"You allude to the fact that you believe that a dog can't be Prime Minister."*
Me: *"What did I say to make you infer such a ludicrous thought?"*
My Dog: *"'Let me be the first person . . . to congratulate you.' You emphasized the word 'person' as if a nonperson can't be Prime Minister."*
Me: *"I think your questionable lack of self-confidence is projecting."*
My Dog: *"Don't start with your babble-talk, George."*
Me: *"Me, babble-talk?"*
My Dog: *"You could just support my decision and leave well enough alone."*
Me: *"Oh?"*
My Dog: *"I have many changes I plan on making when I take on my new leadership position."*
Me: *"Anything you can share?"*
My Dog: *"Well— Aaah, ha! I see what you're doing."*

Me: *"What?"*

My Dog: *"Lull your dog into a false sense of security, encourage your dog who will someday be Prime Minister to discuss his political platform, then use such information to have said dog whisked away and never heard from again."*

Me: *"You're over-thinking."*

My Dog: *"Oh, am I?"*

Me: *"How about a bone?"*

My Dog: *"A bone?"*

Me: *"Yes, a bone."*

My Dog: *"Yeah, a bone would be really nice."*

Me: *"I'll go get it for you, just hang on."*

My Dog: *"Mind if I lick myself here while I'm waiting?"*

Me: *"No, not at all."*

From: **http://www.blogs.es/~christophercolumbus/blog.html**

Subject: **The Quest Continues . . .**

Having found myself with more hours in the day than I know what to do with, I decided it would be worth updating my blog so those following our journey to the Indies since we left Palos on August 3 would have something to consult until official word of our arrival found its way back to Spain.

If you haven't kept up on what I've blogged about over the last twenty days, you can read my previous entries <u>here</u>, <u>here</u>, <u>here</u>, <u>here</u>, <u>here</u>, <u>here</u>, <u>here</u>, <u>here</u>, <u>here</u>, <u>here</u>, <u>here</u>, <u>here</u>, <u>here</u>, <u>here</u>, <u>here</u>, <u>here</u>, <u>here</u>, <u>here</u>, and <u>here</u>. Or I can save you the time and tell you that we have seen . . . **nothing**. Wave after wave obstructs the same view over and over again—that of the horizon. Therefore, it has given me time to thoughtfully explore other subject matter that affects my mood and demeanor.

Yes. Let's talk about the *Niña*, again.

It's important that I explain all the thoughts in my head on the subject (which I have explored for twenty previous entries as well, as there has been nothing else to think about). I command three ships filled with men. We are explorers, sailors and such. There has never been nor will there ever be a little girl on any of my ships so why then name one of these wooden giants "the little girl"?

The *Pinta* or "painted one" and the *Santa María* (which, yes, was originally referred to as "Dirty Mary") are masculine and make total sense for a journey such as this. But "little girl"? Little girl!?

Yes, I do have a lot of spare time on my hands. Yes, I often spend the daylight hours simply drafting our course, making sure we're staying the course, rechecking the course again, announcing to others that yes, we're still on course and then making lists of alternative names for the *Niña*. Here are some that I have come up with over the last twenty days that, I believe, instill respect, honor and fear into those who might come across our bow.

Serpiente (or, Snake)
Tiburón (or, Shark)
Astilla (or, Splinter)
Evil Wooden Ship of Death
Really Bad Evil Wooden Ship of Death (emphasize the "Really Bad" part)
So Bad You Can't Even Imagine, Evil Wooden Ship of Death

With limited food and water (as we are working with rations) I find that my mind is not as sharp as usual, but I do believe that one of the "Wooden Ship of Death" titles would far surpass the silly *Niña* naming scheme, as we are not little girls but grown men.

I will continue to put more thought into this matter and will follow up once again tomorrow with my twenty-second blog entry from my cabin here on the ship.

By the way, we are on course.

From: **http://www.herman_melville.com/~blog/**

Subject: • • •

Call me crazy . . . but having visited the washroom twice earlier, my ears had heard what only now my eyes could confirm. Flipping and flopping around in the sparkling white bowl was a huge black object that most definitely did not belong. Alas, it was encroaching on my simple existence and would have to be dispatched before any more harm could be done.

The invention, of course, of the flushable chamber pot has been around for decades but just recently found its way into the homes of those in the New York City area. Outhouses still reign supreme if not simply being the result of a lack of financial possibility, since the purchasing and installing of such an item can cost more than one expects.

My fears, of course, were apparent; there being a certain goal in mind when I found myself behind closed doors and ready to unleash what "once was" into the twisting pipes below my house. Yet, knowing that somewhere in the water lurked a foreign creature with the ability to snap at me while I sat, caused my thoughts to turn toward eradication before evacuation. There being nothing worse than being blind while exposed, the solution was evident.

Still in its infancy, the sewer systems set up for the country and outerlying areas of New York City are far from perfection. With limited areas set aside for the disposal of such household remnants, and a limited amount of service personnel available to assist in such matters, it often surprises one just how little there is to be done when the mechanics behind the new technology do not function correctly or altogether back up.

Of course, before sitting down to do my prearranged business, I had to do away with the foreign creature that had obviously set his sights on disrupting my peace. I stood above the wavering pool of water, peering into the depths for a quick glance at that which was pursuing me. In fact, I was pursuing the creature, being the heathen that I was, in an attempt to put an end to the terror it had caused as of late. The rubber plunger, attached to the side of the mechanism, would cause the undoing of the mysterious black insect.

As quickly as I could, I lifted up the instrument while purposefully jabbing the side of the ceramic structure with force . . . causing the monstrous creature to emerge once again from the depths of the darkened hole at the base of the bowl. I jammed the object, gripped tightly in my hand again and again. I stabbed; for hate's sake. Spit my last breath at the blackened creature. Eyes matched for a moment, as our souls connected in this battle of wills.

In the process, liquid splashed and spilled forth upon the tile floor, causing gravity to take hold and flip me on my back, my leg bending beneath me. The room went dark, much like the mask of the evil creature, and I awoke hours later with my leg lifted high above the bed.

As I will be here for some time, leg tied and courage battered—I suspect I will continue to elaborate on my quest to do away with that which caused me this pain.

Revenge will be mine. That much I will see to.

In the meantime, if you're interested you can purchase my latest books <u>here</u> and <u>here</u>.

From: **http://www.thomaspaine.com/**

Subject: **Self-Publishing!**

With the current state of the Revolutionary War, things are in dire straits—these are the motivating factors that urged me to draft my latest document denouncing British rule.

I have mentioned this document before, as I have been working on the writing of said document for many weeks now. But as I am close to releasing this document to the public via this blog, I am striving to come up with a title for such prose.

That is why I look to you, dear readers, for your creative insight and influence. This document needs a title that is simple, yet communicates clearly. It should not need explaining or discussion. It should stand on its own. As I mentioned before, this document outlines the reasons why Britain should not be ruling our continent and why this nation is not a "British nation" (this country is composed of influences from all of Europe) and should therefore not be ruled by one.

It is a heady, passionate, important document whose title must reflect such emotions. If you would be so kind, please vote in the below poll, so that I may pick the best title prior to releasing the PDF and Audiobook versions to the public at large.

Time is of the essence! Also, if you have other ideas not on this list, please <u>e-mail me</u> with them.

Thomas Paine's Untitled Document Should Be Called:

- **IT'S LIKE, SOMETHING WE ALL KNOW**
- **ALL ON THE SAME PAGE: MY THOUGHTS ON THE SUBJECT**
- **THIRTEEN COLONIES: THIRTEEN PROBLEMS**
- **IT'S THERE, IN YOUR HEAD, THAT INFORMATION**
- **YOUR FATHER SHOULD HAVE TAUGHT YOU THIS**
- **WHO LIKES THE BRITISH? NOT ME, THOMAS PAINE!**
- **GO AWAY, REDCOATS!**
- **UNCOMMON THOUGHTS FOR A COMMON PROBLEM**
- **THE REDCOATS: NOT WELL READ**
- **WHY IT ALL MAKES SENSE TO US COMMON FOLK**
- **T STANDS FOR "TEA" BUT ALSO FOR "TROUBLE"**
- **WAR SPELLED BACKWARDS IS "RAW," WHICH IS HOW WE'RE ALL PROBABLY FEELING RIGHT ABOUT NOW DUE TO THIS ANNOYING BRITISH RULE THING**
- **WHAT YOU'RE ABOUT TO READ, YOU PROBABLY ALREADY KNOW, BUT ISN'T IT TIME WE ALL READ WHAT WE ALREADY KNOW SO WE CAN AGREE ABOUT THE SUBJECTS CONTAINED THEREIN?**

From: **http://www.blogs.fr/~vangogh/**
Subject: **Elements of a Painting**

Thank you all for your interest as of late in my paintings—things have been extremely tough, as I have chosen a profession that often does not reward talent with financial stability. These days it seems that people only believe my paintings are worth the value of the paint on the canvas, while I would have hoped that others could have seen the beauty and value within each frozen moment that I have gazed upon and re-created.

Nevertheless, it is okay. Some of you have asked what I find beautiful. Where my images come from. I have said before and will say it again—first I dream my dreams, and then I paint them. Everything comes from within, and beauty is, indeed, in the eye of the beholder.

Personally, I find beauty in the natural moments around us. The stars in the sky. A flower in a vase. The human face, i.e., the nose, ears and mouth. There can be beauty in most anything, and as long as one finds something worth looking at, there are bound to be others.

Which brings me to the art of shaving.

I find that shaving is a very complicated job that requires the steadiest of hands. It's ironic, that my hands can hold a paintbrush without a tremor, yet when I bring a blade up to the side of my beard, my digits shake with terror. It's amazing to watch, as the hand holding said blade jerks back and forth as if it has a mind of its own. It has often made it hard to shave my beard, and one of the reasons I leave it intact.

This week, however, I plan on shaving my beard completely off—and trimming my sideburns from next to my ears. As my great-nephew will be visiting, I would like to present myself in a far more conservative light as opposed to the manner in which I portray myself when I am alone, working solitarily. If you must know, the last time my great-nephew visited me I was tired, unshaven and slovenly—it scared him to see me in such a state of disarray.

That is why I have decided to snip the problem before he arrives, and allow the two of us to bond as I had hoped the previous visit—a great-uncle and his great-nephew, two clean-cut relatives, comfortable with each other in each and every way.

You'll probably never recognize me when I'm done!

From: **http://www.maryshelley.blog/**

Subject: **Writer's Block**

You may remember my writings of <u>last week</u> in which I told you of the unique writing exercise I took part in with fellow literates like Dr. John Polidori. A ghost story was the goal, and I was surprisingly dry of inspiration.

Yesterday evening, still desperate for such inspiration, I made my way to a local café where I sat with my journal, scribbling notes. For most of the evening, things were quiet indeed, and I found myself wrapping things up as the sun began to set.

That was just about the time that "he" walked in.

Filled with liquor and the accompanying stench to prove it, the most uncoordinated human being I have ever seen pushed his way in through the doors to the establishment. He was knocking over chairs and tables and moaning incoherent phrases that no one could understand. Even for me, sitting at a corner table, his glazed eyes and hulking stature caused me to gather my things and retreat to the other side of the café.

As he entered the establishment he knocked two candles off a nearby table, sending them crashing to the floor and lighting a small curtain on fire—which fell and caused the man to scream in a rage that terrified most of us. His coordination faltering, the man landed headfirst on yet another table, sending him crashing to the floor where he remained quiet from that point forward.

The waiter informed me that this drunkard, Franco, was often getting himself into trouble the likes of which no one had ever seen—and that he was homeless and without family, often wandering the streets looking for someone or something to take him in.

It was sad, of course, and it caused me to think for a moment about what it means to belong.

Nonetheless, after things calmed, I found my way back home where I continued to try and come up with a story for this ridiculous literary challenge. And still, here I sit, without a subject, story or even an engaging character around which I could fashion a story.

Maybe a good night's rest will do my creative mind some good.

From: http://www.julius_caesar.com/

Subject: Thoughts of March

As I write this, I ready my campaign against Parthia—a victory that, if achieved, will bring Rome the wealth it once had and lost. I find myself confident that such a campaign will be successful, bringing not just me but all Romans the spoils of victory. Talk of this will do us no good as its success is already guaranteed by the almighty Jupiter.

Instead, let's talk about some of my cohorts for a moment.

Specifically, I speak of Gaius Trebonius, Gaius Cassius Longinus and my cousin Marcus Brutus. The other evening we were all sitting out under the stars talking of our past triumphs together and the future to come.

I recall saying to Brutus that I found myself looking to the month of April. That once March passed and the campaign against Parthia began . . . that April should be a very pleasant month.

Yet Brutus simply said, *"Yeah, not so much."*

I turned to Gaius Cassius and asked him if he might desire sharing a meal with me back at the palace—and he asked when. After telling him that such a date should occur within the next seven days, he replied, *"Dear Caesar . . . why don't we wait to make plans until, well, more time has passed?"*

First Brutus had no love of April. Then Gaius wanted to wait until more time has passed to share a meal together? I turned to the last of my three, Gaius Trebonius, and asked him if, possibly, he wanted to go hunting the following week. His response?

"Ask me in April."

I paused, eyeing all three of the men at my side. And with my forceful voice I demanded to know what was going on.

At first, the looks on their faces were taut—but then, smiles all around. These three men, whose careers had advanced and whose previously murderous activities had been pardoned by yours truly . . . Caesar, suddenly began . . . one by one . . . to laugh.

First, Gaius Cassius, then Trebonius, and finally Brutus. Laughter all around. It seemed as if the joke was on me.

I said, *"Even you, Brutus?"*

The men by my side, those who surround me and support me, had fooled me with their innocent joke.

"You guys . . ." I said, scolding their practical joke.

They laughed some more and more and more until they couldn't laugh anymore. It was, to say the least, a humorous and lighthearted evening from then on.

From: **http://www.buster_keaton.com/blog/**

Subject: ⎯

At a loss for words, today.

From: **http://www.blogs.com/~l_ron.hubbard/**

Subject: **On Stands Now!**

Today marks an exciting milestone for yours truly.

My latest novel, *Final Blackout,* which many of you have heard me mention in previous posts, is now available for order. You can, of course, go to a store and buy it there but if you order now from the link at the left—you'll get a very special edition of the book from yours truly and you don't have to give your money away to the corporate bigwigs. Buy it <u>here</u>.

For those who don't know, *Final Blackout* takes place in a futuristic world ravaged by thirty years of war and centers on the main character known simply as "The Lieutenant." Well, who is he? He's charismatic. A leader. A statesman. The only man who is capable of taking power away from those who have gained control in less than appealing ways. The book is getting a great deal of good reviews, great press, and a huge 100,000-copy first printing, which means it's got to be good.

Funnily enough, one of my friends had read an early copy of the book and called me on the phone to discuss it the other day. His comments were glowing, of course, and he spent a lot of time praising the core theme of the book—that one man can, indeed, against insurmountable odds, do absolutely anything he sets his mind to. That one man, if he appears crazily passionate enough, can convince a world of people to follow him in his cause no matter how insane or silly that cause may appear on the surface!

Then he joked and said that it almost felt like a religion unto itself!

We laughed about it for a few minutes, the fact that modeling any kind of religious following based on themes from a science fiction book would just be plain silly. We talked about how hilarious it might have been had people modeled a religion after H. G. Wells's book *War of the Worlds*—you know, a religion that would be based on the theme of strange alien creatures that must be eradicated or else humans would suffer! A religion based on getting rid of aliens! Hah!

We must have laughed for hours as we went through a variety of well-known pieces of literature, turning each one into our own wacky religion. It was entertaining, to say the least.

Nonetheless, I digress.

So, don't forget to visit the L. Ron Hubbard Online Store and purchase my latest book so that I am able to continue to bring you the quality science fiction literature that all of you have grown to expect.

Thanks for all your support!

From: **http://www.marilynmonroe.com/~blog/**

Subject: **Grrrr!**

I hate J. I hate him I hate him I hate him I hate him I hate him.

There I said it.

Well, I didn't say it. I typed it. But you know what I mean.

Why do guys have to always be so all about themselves? Why do they have to put their work above the women they love? It's always the same thing. Mostly, with J, he's just so obsessed with his work that I can hardly ever steal away time with him. Sometimes, it feels like he's trying so hard to control the world around him that he never has time for me. Sneaking around, late night calls—I don't know, but I don't always feel like I'm his primary focus. If you can't meet me at a nice restaurant for a nice dinner out with the rest of the town . . . If you have to meet me at a hotel at 1 am in the morning, well, there's something definitely wrong with our relationship.

I mean, it seems that way, doesn't it?

Thanks for all the great e-mails and support. Frank and Eloise were right when they e-mailed to tell me to forget about J. That if he really loved me he'd make the time and stop all these excuses about "important meetings" and "world-shaping decisions." I mean, c'mon—who tells their girlfriend that they can't meet up because of something going on in Cuba.

Cuba!? It's not even like he was going to Cuba.

It's obvious, isn't it. I am so stupid. One of those girls, you know? So head over heels for J. Why do I always have to do this? Why do I always fall for the assholes? The guys who treat me like a piece of garbage and walk all over me? I don't deserve this. Really, I don't. I'm a good girl. Well, you know what I mean.

E-mail me and tell me if you think I should stay with J. If more people say I should stay with J than people telling me not to, I'll take that as a sign. If more people say I should break up with J, then . . . Well, then I'll think about breaking up with J. If it's equal on both sides, then I'll wait and see how this week goes.

I hate him I hate him I hate him.

From: **http://www.leonardo-davinci.com/class_notes.html**
Subject: **Four Years ... in the Making**

Students looking for the annual list of assignments and lectures should be looking <u>here</u>. Students looking for this week's current assignment can surf <u>here</u>. All other class-related questions can be directed to <u>leo@davinci.com</u>.

I'd like to take this week's entry to talk about our ongoing class project that has finally just been completed. Back in 1503 I decided that not only should I teach students how to find their own creative vision, but also how to work in groups to complete a collective piece of artwork. It was then that we began this "untitled project" and my group of students that year decided on the direction of the piece of art.

Dubbed *Lady on Canvas*, students in my '03 class never got around to painting anything resembling a woman at all. By the end of classes that year, the collective work resembled a backdrop of sorts. Columns, mountain trails and greenery. View the artwork from '03 <u>here</u>.

Students in my '04 seminar began working on the collective project halfway through the season, each taking turns adding depth, color and dimension to the project, which eventually resulted in the image of a young man's face looking out from the center of the canvas. Some joked tht the young man's face resembled that of a pious Jesus Christ, so in response, students mischievously painted ambiguous and meaningless codes and riddles into the piece, then changed the name from *Lady on Canvas* to *Decapitated Male Head Floating Above the Mountains*. So amusing. A snapshot of the project at this point in the exercise is <u>here</u>.

My '05 class, unhappy with the artistic direction of this collective work, painted over elements of the '03 and '04 students, changing the man's face into that of a homely woman's face which happened to resemble that of our very own Italian student, Lisa. Thus, it made total sense for '05 students to rename the project, *Lisa Abroad, in the Mountains of Ether*. Now completed, <u>the project</u> represents almost three years in the making, and proves the point that a piece of art is never finished—it is always evolving.

It also just goes to show you—it takes many to create a singular piece of flawless art.

Since my students completed the collective work, I have framed it in an ornate gold housing, hanging it in my home. You can see it in all its glory <u>here</u> and <u>here</u>. For a project completed over all those years, by all those people, *Lisa Abroad, in the Mountains of Ether* is, in my opinion—a true collective masterpiece.

One that each and every student should receive notoriety from.

From: **http://www.jessiejames.com/~blog/**

Subject: **Linky Love . . .**

The gang's been busy lately and we've been riding west—looks like we're about comin' up on Missouri soon where we've got some business to take care of if ya know what I mean. Meantime, wanted to give a holler to my boys who all have these writin' spaces of their own where they talk about their thoughts and stuff.

Also cuz they keep harassin' me about telling you all about their spaces cuz people come here to see what the great Jessie James is doin' but never go to their spaces—so those whining dogs have finally gotten what was comin' to them. Go to their space and look around or I'll shoot ya! Hah. Just kidding.

<u>Frank James:</u> My bro. Loves animals. Loves to shoot 'em. Talks about shootin' animals on his scribblin' space. Shot a deer last week. Loved that too. He got a <u>picture</u> of it up there if you wanna see it.

<u>Bob Younger:</u> Brother of Cole and James. Likes shootin' stuff too. But not animals. Hates snakes. Afraid of 'em. He's got a horse too. His horse hates snakes also. Would rather shoot you than eat vegetables.

<u>Cole Younger:</u> Loves gold. Loves guns. Loves shooting if it means it'll get him some gold. Wrote a poem about gold and it's on his site. Pretty inspirin'.

<u>James Younger:</u> Can hold two guns at once. Loves to tell you that he can, even though everyone else has two hands and can do the same thing. Don't kid him about it or he'll shoot ya. Loves to shoot his gun like the rest of the boys. Hates his last name and will shoot you if you make fun of it.

<u>Bill Chadwell, Clell Miller and Charlie Pitts:</u> These guys all love shooting their guns off and if it involves robbin' and stuff they're happier than pigs in mud. Don't believe in shooting anyone in the back—that's just plain criminal. Good guys, these three.

Look forward to any comments from all you readers out there. No one seems to want to leave comments ever since that one guy left a negative comment and, well, you know what happened.

I just want to promise all of you that it will never happen again! I'm working through the anger issues and welcome your thoughts on my writin' space and my boys' writin' spaces!

Serious! What d'ya all think about my writin' space here!?

From: **http://www.donnerfamily.com/~george_donner/blog.html**

Subject: **Heading West!**

On behalf of the entire Donner family, I'm logging our last post before we leave Illinois for the West Coast. With us comes the Reed family and their hired hands—in total, the party ends up at around thirty-one individuals. Hello to all of you reading this entry!

You should know, I took a peek at the food we'll be bringing along for the trip and it is mmm, mmm good! Beef and flour and other yummy bits of rations not only make my stomach rumble, but make me long for those warm nights under the starry sky, singing songs and sharing ourselves with each other.

There's nothing like the excitement of a new beginning. Of taking a minor, if not tiny little risk, to live a better life in California! Where it's sunny and the weather is great and both families (Reed and Donner) can learn to depend on each other's skills and dedication. Remember, it's what's on someone's inside that counts! In our toughest times over the course of the next few weeks that's something we should all remember.

Look within and take advantage of that! I know I will!

My wife asked me what I was looking forward to the most over the course of the next few weeks, and I must say it's the hunkering down and spending some isolated, quiet time with the rest of our party. You know, finding a shelter, making camp and not having to deal with any other people in the world. An experience like that, where it's just us and no one else for miles, to me, seems like paradise! Here's to something just like that!

I'll be checking back in with you at various points during the trip, but if you don't hear from me it just means that we're having a wonderful, successful and productive good time and we'll contact each other as soon as we find a place to settle in!

E-mail me with any questions!

From: **http://www.jimhenson.com/~ blog/**
Subject: **Another One Bites the Dust . . .**

Yet another relationship . . . down the tubes.

G sat me down this past weekend after six months of being together and told me that she no longer wanted us to see each other. That she just felt like we weren't connecting and that our backgrounds were different. This, of course, is something I've heard before and I never asked questions—I always accepted the outcome. But not this time. I wasn't going to let another relationship end without finding out the exact reason why.

I pushed G over and over again until she finally broke and told me.

No, it wasn't that we weren't connecting. It wasn't that our backgrounds were different. It didn't even have to do with her not being attracted to me or not liking my family. When it came down to it, it was all about one silly little misunderstanding.

My socks.

Weeks prior, apparently G had seen me with my hands in my socks. Talking to my socks with my hands in them. She, well, told me that "it made her a little bit uncomfortable," and that since the initial incident she had seen me doing it every time I made my way past the chest of drawers in my bedroom.

To be fair to her, yes. I have done this. Why? I'm not quite sure, although deep down I feel a compulsion to do so. I've done the research, I've read books—and nowhere have I seen an explanation of such a thing. So my hands are in a sock. So I talk to them. Is there anything really so wrong with that? Is it something to end a relationship over?

I expressed these thoughts to G, who was adamant that she couldn't see past this "obvious fetish" I seemed to have with socks. Another relationship down the drain.

On the bright side (because there always is one if you really look deep inside yourself), I now have more time to get to know myself and what's inside.

Someday I'll find it. That obvious connection. The lovers, the dreamers and me.

From: **http://www.lincolnblog.com/forum/**

Subject: **Today's Thoughts on the Lincoln Blog Discussion Forum's Vulgar Commentators**

Seven months ago my webmaster brought forth on this blog a new forum section, dedicated to the proposition that all men should be given equality in public discussion. Yet now it seems that the users are engaged in a great war of words, testing whether this forum or any forum so dedicated can long endure.

We are met on a great blog forum of that war of words, having come to dedicate a portion of that forum as a final resting place for posts and opinions and rants for as long as this blog forum might exist. It is altogether fitting and proper that we should do this.

But in a large sense, we cannot fully alleviate such vulgar words here on this site. Brave men, who struggled here in this blog forum for goodness, have added, not detracted, to the overall power of the typewritten word. It is the "bad apples" who have detracted by spreading rumors about my private life, twisting my words and the words of my family, and by posting unflattering, unclothed pictures of Mary Todd Lincoln that strangely have never existed prior to this forum's existence. The world will little note nor long remember what we say or do here in this forum, but that which is not remembered must still be presented respectfully.

We must be dedicated to the great task remaining before us—that these vulgar commentators who put forth unnecessary and harmful words should be reported and removed from the Lincoln blog as to present the rest of our users with a new birth of freedom—a blog forum of the members, by the members and for the members.

When such has been realized, only then will the Lincoln blog's forum section be a true testament to the users of this weblog.

--

In other news, I will be attending a performance of *Our American Cousin* at the Ford Theatre this week! If you plan on also attending, please stop by and say hello! I hear the performers are truly passionate about their craft!

From: **http://www.tutankhamen.com/**
Subject: **Rules, Schmules!**

The 1330s sure are boring.

You'd think there'd be something better to do around here than just sit in my room, but my advisor Ay, along with the others, suggest that I be heard but not seen. Instilling fear in and gaining respect from Egyptians for a boy my age is a tough prospect and must be, as Ay says, handled delicately.

But I am soooooooo bored.

I asked Ay when I would be able to start making decisions on my own and he suggested that when I had lived twenty-one years, that then, then I could be allowed such privileges. Same old story—as long as I live in this kingdom, I must follow his laws. Only by following his laws will everyone else fear me. Fear. That is power, he says.

I started to think about fears. The kinds of things that I'm afraid of. Here's some that I came up with:

First of all, I am afraid of being confined in small dark places. Anything where I can't really move, or where I have to lie in a position where my arms are crossed over my chest and my legs must remain straight. Or anything where my face is covered with something. That gives me the willies.

Secondly, you wouldn't believe this, but I am afraid of being the center of attention. You know, people looking at me, peering into my eyes. I can imagine that the most horrific thing ever would be to have to stand somewhere, still, and just let thousands of people stand and stare at me. That makes my skin crawl.

Finally, and this is silly because I am so young and have so many years ahead of me— but I would wish that when my time does come that people remember me in respectful ways. Perhaps if someone would write a song about me, something that remembers my years as King . . . Something that really takes my rule seriously and presents me in a respectful light . . . That would be good. Thinking about the years after my life, and not being treated with such lyrical respect, is a fear of mine.

Oh well. Thank Osiris I'll never have to worry about those things!!

From: http://www.antonio_salieri.com/mozartbootlegs/

Subject: Mozart Bootlegs

Amadeus Mozart would have you think that in order to experience "the grandeur" of his performances, that you must either be a royal or have the financial resources to attend one of his concerts.

That is why I started my Mozart bootleg site—so "peons," as Mozart would refer to you, would have an opportunity to listen to his music and make up their own mind about whether or not the composer really is as good as he says he is. (The answer is no.)

Nonetheless, I have kept a fairly exhaustive collection of his performances (along with some brief personal comments of my own) in an attempt to better my own techniques (and to be aware of the mistakes and pitfalls such a composer falls into when he is more interested in his image than his music). Also, if you see Mozart doing anything stupid, please e-mail me with the information so I may post it on my Stupid Things Mozart Did This Week website.

Performances/Bootlegs:

In the Court of the Elector of Bavaria (he stutters at 01:18:33)	1762
Imperial Court (played same note twice at 00:07:11)	1762
Court of Munich (snorted while playing at 02:00:23)	1763
Court of Mannheim (long pause at 00:34:33)	1763
Court of Paris (song played out of order, first 30 seconds!)	1763
Court of London (just plain bad, 00:00:00–2:31:00)	1763
The Hague (sounded a little off, 01:11:09)	1764
Three Nights in Paris (fully out of tune, which is Mozart's fault)	1764
Salzburg #1 (finger slippage on keys at 00:25:21)	1768
Salzburg #2 (first night was better)	1768
Salzburg #3 (not nearly as good as second night)	1768

Click above to download. Please share with anyone you like! Comments and questions to salieri@hatemozart.com.

From: **http://www.andy_warhol.com/blog/**

Subject: **My Blog Entry**

MY BLOG ENTRY

m y b l o g e n t r y

MY BLOG ENTRY

m y b l o g e n t r y

MY BLOG ENTRY

my blog entry

my blog entry

MY BLOG ENTRY

MY BLOG ENTRY

MY BLOG ENTRY

From: **http://www.betsy-ross.com/~sewingblog/**
Subject: **Patriotic Projects**

Greetings fellow sewers, knitters and others with artistic trades! Back by popular demand, this week I'd like to highlight a selection of very creative projects I've worked up for all of you! Please note, by clicking on a project, you will be charged a nominal fee for the pattern, instructions and the Betsy Ross trademark logo.

Star-Spangled Winter Cap
Warm, snuggly and patriotic! This star-spangled winter cap incorporates the famous Betsy Ross American Flag theme, while giving mothers and grandmothers the opportunity to craft something to keep their man's head warm out on cold nights while fighting the British!

Red, White and Blue Bonnet
For Sundays at Church or for those nice family picnics, what better way to show your support for Betsy Ross and our Founding Fathers than to wear the famous Betsy Ross American Flag theme on a silk, stylish bonnet? (Also available—Star-Spangled Bonnet)

13 Star Suspenders
Does your husband have trouble keeping his pants up? Why not sew him a pair of suspenders, decorated with the thirteen stars representing the thirteen colonies, as made famous by Betsy Ross!? Now your man can be popular, patriotic—and the "star" of your city or town. Comes with bonus red, white and blue wooden teeth! (Also available—13 Star Stockings)

Patriotic Pants w/ Red Ruffles
Betsy Ross's trademark patriotic pants which she wore while crafting America's greatest visual treat can be yours with this easy-to-follow, easy-to-sew pattern. What woman wouldn't love to wear these airy and baggy pants, covered in stars and stripes, and made even more appealing with a red ruffle trim! Betsy Ross knows how it feels, and soon so shall you!

Absolutely Amazing Apron
It's an apron. And it's absolutely amazing due to the red, white and blue colored squares, all surrounding the face of the famous Betsy Ross! Show your friends you

know who's responsible for America's greatest sewn icon, the American flag, by wearing this amazing accoutrement while preparing meals for your family! (Also available—<u>Absolutely Amazing Army Pants</u>)

Hope you all enjoy the above patterns and projects! Stay tuned for further projects, so you can be the "spangled star" of your town!

From: **http://georgeburns.blogs.com/**

Subject: **If You Can Read This, Your Eyesight Is Better than Mine**

I need a magnifying glass to see what I am typing up here. Which of course, is a much better alternative than women needing a magnifying glass to see what I am hyping down there . . . Yet here I sit, mostly because I can't stand . . . writing to you.

People told me this blog thing was a great way to pick up women. At the insane asylum. See, it's the people who spend all day in a dark room that scare me—mostly because I just don't have the stamina for that anymore. Seriously, though—I figure that this is a great way to be remembered . . . until all the electricity goes out.

Maybe after I'm dead, which some people think I am already, people will turn on their computers (if they can figure out how to) and tune in to this place. I've always wanted to leave something behind for the American public. Besides my cold, lifeless, very attractive body.

I hope I wrote something funny up there. Can you see it? I can't.

Personally, I don't believe in dying. It's been done. I'm working on a new exit. Besides, I can't die now—you're here, reading me. Or sleeping. Either way, you're a captive audience. I always said that a comedian's best tools are his sense of humor and a roll of duct tape. Pretty sticky sis!

I wanted to take the opportunity today to talk about something extremely important and historically significant, so I decided to talk about me.

Some more.

I don't quite get this e-mail thing. An electronic way of sending mail in seconds. I don't want to do anything that only takes seconds. I'd rather not even have a quick wit. When you get to be my age, you want everything slower. Aging, sex and sponge baths from the nurses. I like nurses. Anyone who changes your diaper can't be all that bad.

Okay, time's up. Gotta go. If you want to e-mail me, you can send your hate mail here, but remember that since I hate e-mail, I'll never read it.

See you next week!

G.

From: **http://www.sittingbull-onlinepoker.com/**

Subject: **Sitting Bull's Online Poker Emporium and Blog Is Currently Closed**

Currently engaged in battle against General Custer. Will reopen as soon as humanly possible.

From: **http://www.lyndon_b_johnson.com/blog/**

Subject: **A Thousand Thanks!**

Lady Bird and I wanted to thank everyone for their support this week in the election—your involvement, dedication and support to both my family and President-elect Kennedy will not go unnoticed. There's a lot that President Kennedy and myself want to do for the American people and we're looking forward to getting our hands dirty—if you know what I mean.

This week brought back many memories for Lady Bird and myself from the Senate days—and while my victory back then in becoming a Texas senator was widely known to be a slim victory separated by just a few votes—the rumors of this week's election being won by a small margin is neither here nor there. The American people have spoken, and I am proud to be a part of that choice.

As I promised during the middle of the campaign, I will answer a limited amount of questions via e-mail. This week's question comes from jimmyp13@aol.com who asks, *"How does it feel to be the Vice President of the United States!?"*

Well, Jimmy—although I am not technically the Vice President of the United States just yet, I must say that it makes me feel honored and relieved all at once. Honored that I was offered the position by President-elect Kennedy, and accepted by the American public. Relieved in that the position is not that of the President.

You must know, as your teachers have taught you in school, the job of President of the United States is a huge job. It is a position that is unforgiving. Mistakes cannot happen. Decisions must be made without any wavering. Other world leaders look to our President in shaping their own policies. As Vice President, I will fortunately not have to deal with as much pressure and responsibility.

Can I just say, "phew"? Seriously, really—I'm a bit relieved.

The next e-mail question comes from abagail88@dc.com who asks, *"Do you think you'll run for President at the end of your term as Vice President?"*

Well, Abagail—let me just answer that quickly by saying that although it may very well be a possibility, it is a possibility that is very very very very very far off and something that I won't have to worry about for at least two–three years. And for that, I am thankful!

Although someday, maybe, possibly—I could be interested in a position such as that, it's good to know that for now, I can learn from President-elect Kennedy in this "apprentice" type position, where the American public will not rely as heavily on me as they will on the President of the United States!

With that being said, I want to thank everyone again for their support and I look forward to being the best Vice President for this country that I can be!

From: **http://www.helenkeller.com/~photoblog/**

Outdoor shot at Ivy Green Estate during wintertime.

Me and fellow students at Wright-Humason School for the Deaf in NYC.

Sunset and mountain range, Alabama.

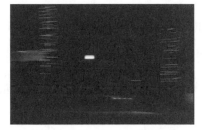

Nightlife in Connecticut, 1948.

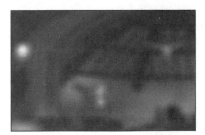

Church, I think.

Family picnic and day of fun!

From: **http://www.lewisandclarkexpedition.com/ ~meriwetherlewis/**

Subject: **Personal Web Journal, Entry #47**

Let me ask you a question.

If you've been chosen to lead an expedition to the West Coast of the Americas by the President of the United States himself, and you stick your neck out (and even lie) so that a friend of yours with a much lower rank (i.e., Second Lieutenant) can co-lead such an expedition, and you even go out of your way to refer to him as Captain even though he's never even held the rank of Captain . . . Don't you think that if his whistling is getting on your nerves and you ask him to stop whistling even though the Indians seem to like the whistling (which he'll continue to tell you over and over and over again) . . . that he should stop the whistling?

It's not that I abhor whistling. Before the Corps of Discovery left Saint Charles, Missouri, for the West Coast, I often found myself whistling in times of relaxation and thoughtfulness. But whistling the **same song** (<u>MP3 link here</u>), over and over and over again, over the course of five months, and giving such an invented song a title like "The Whistling Walk" and insisting on learning how to translate that into a variety of native languages just so you can make sure they know the name in their own tongues is, well, annoying.

And while I'm on the subject of whistling, I'd also like to ask you a second question. If you've been chosen by the Captain of a high-profile exploration mission to the West Coast and he sticks out his neck for you and even refers to you as Captain in front of all the other Privates on such an exploration, and one day you ask to borrow your friend/Captain's rifle to kill an animal . . . And during the process of killing such an animal you get dirt and gunk in the trigger . . . And your Captain/friend asks you to clean out the trigger area so it doesn't rust . . . And you tell him you will . . . And then you never do it . . . And you get asked again every day for two months to clean out the trigger and you still don't do it . . . Don't you consider that to be, well, wrong?

And don't get me started on the coughing of one fellow Captain, who also loves to tell stories that have **no endings whatsoever,** tries to make leadership decisions and proclamations that are obviously not his own, expects that he should be the liaison between President Jefferson and all Indians for the sole reason that he knows French (which doesn't even have any bearing on the situation) and that he should also get the most of a meal because he needs more energy, which will help him in his leadership techniques when, in fact, he has no leadership techniques whatsoever.

I think that's all I have to say today.

From: **http://www.lewisandclarkexpedition.com/ ~williamclark/**

Subject: **Personal Web Journal, Entry #47**

Things are going so great!

I can't express how great things are going here in our exploration to the West Coast of the Americas. Really, being Captain of the expedition has been both enlightening and exciting, since every single member of my team looks up to me as the ultimate leader of this trip!

I have a story to share with all our readers, which I think will be extremely telling and exciting to all of you who are keeping up here on the <u>Corps of Discovery Weblogs</u>. Having met the Yankton Indians, our group decided to sit down with their governing council in an attempt to inform them that this land, now, belonged to the United States. We were, as instructed, ready to offer such natives the protection and trade agreements in exchange for the safety of the land when something very insane happened—

On a totally unrelated note, "The Whistling Walk" has now become the favorite whistle song of the entire company—and although I seem to be the only one capable of fully whistling all thirty-two bars of the song over and over again without ever getting tired, I can see that the expedition has benefited from such happy, high-spirited, musical accompaniment.

Really, there's not much more I have to say! Things are going great and I'm having a great time and morale between Lewis and myself couldn't possibly be any better!

I'll respond to questions whenever possible! Just be sure to <u>e-mail</u> all your questions to me. Meriwether really doesn't have the time to deal with that. So, just be sure to send them to me.

From: **http://www.freud-blog.com**

Subject: **Self-Analysis, Dream Evaluation #33**

A curious dream awoke me this morning—one filled with images of death and destruction.

With my subconscious at the helm, the dream presented me with an image of myself as a child, standing atop a large cliff and looking down at the unforgiving waters of the ocean. There I stood for some time. Staring out as the wind whipped violently against my face. I was holding hands with someone, whose face was obscured by the blurred vision—most likely the result of my subconscious not wanting to reveal who, as a child, I desired to be with in life and singularly in death.

Then, without warning, the body of my younger self went limp, letting go of the safe hand and falling and twisting out of control to the murky waters below. Upon hitting the waters, however, I did not awaken as most would expect. Instead, a vision of a dark underwater area became clear to me as a variety of faceless other children came into focus.

I awoke with a start upon seeing such faceless children, and can only imagine that these were the children of my youth that I have forgotten—my subconscious trying to communicate with my conscious mind that my memory continues to erase images and faces at an alarming pace.

Posted by S. Freud at 4:11 AM | Permalink | Comments (9)

COMMENTS

Maybe you're afraid of death and destruction.

Posted by: Anonymous | 4:15 AM

Maybe you didn't notice the fact that I didn't ask for observations or interpretations?

Posted by: S. Freud | 4:28 AM

Dreams about falling mean that you're afraid of taking some kind of big step or making some big decision. Maybe you're afraid of something? Afraid that you can't accomplish certain goals in life?

Posted by: Bernard | 7:01 AM

Perhaps you are a scared little bunny rabbit inside that body of yours, afraid that YOU will never live up to your own goals and the only way in which you can make yourself feel more confident is to redirect your energy into convincing others that they, themselves, are not reaching their goals. I say you do not know what you are talking about and should go spend more time with your mother, if you get my gist.

Posted by: S. Freud | 8:21 AM

Can you hold your breath underwater? 'Cause maybe if you can't that's what your dream is telling you, that you're afraid of having to hold your breath underwater. I think that's got to be it, I'm sure of it.

Posted by: Julianne F. | 9:23 AM

This dream is not about holding one's breath underwater. Come back to this blog when you actually have real-world knowledge to contribute!

Posted by: S. Freud | 9:41 AM

I heard that if you dream of faceless children you may be allergic to beets.

Posted by: Gil | 10:01 AM

Please, no more inane comments or observations.

Posted by: S. Freud | 10:21 AM

You have a lot of anger issues, don't you?

Posted by: JD | 11:49 AM

COMMENTS CLOSED

From: **http://www.nostradamus.com/~blog/**
Subject: **Predictions, About Tomorrow's Blog Entry**

Herein, I present to all of you (those who I expected would be here and who I predicted yesterday would arrive today) my predictions for tomorrow's blog posting in typical quatrains, or four-line poetic fashion.

Hundreds of words, flock to the page.
Invisible at first, then plain to the eye.
Sections, paragraphs and quatrains.
Thousands will come for predictions.

Tomorrow, of course, we shall see if the above prediction comes true (which we know it will). My vision of words appearing on this page which were once invisible—and the thousands who will read such words . . . I believe there is no question that this prediction is completely true.

Now, my predictions about the day after tomorrow's blog post:

Letters will form words.
What was once there, will be replaced.
Sentences, phrases and poetry.
Thousands will come, once again, like lambs to the slaughter.

I believe that the above prediction will also come true (although you shall see when the day after tomorrow comes). I will let the words speak for themselves.

I would also like to share with you a prediction I cast a mere seven days ago, in an attempt to answer correspondence and a challenge from a loyal blog reader. Ysidra22@fr.com asked me to predict what I would be doing exactly seven days in the future. Here is what I wrote:

A question is asked.
An answer is given.

Seven days forward, all questions moot.
For Lamus will be revealed as true.

For those confounded with the meaning, I will spell it out as always. Ysidra's question was asked seven days prior. And such questions no longer matter seven days forward since the answer would be given. All this has come true as I am currently answering the seven-day-old question and the question no longer matters. As for this name Lamus, it rhymes with Damus, which happens to be the last part of my name—which must refer to me, Nostradamus, which in turn proves that I am true and honest in my predictions.

That is all for now! I will see you again tomorrow, as I have already predicted.

From: **http://www.benedict_arnold.us.gov/blog/**

Subject: **Bene-DICT is Bene-DOOCED**

When I started this blog during Christmas 1775, I expected it would bring great things to my life. Not what befell me on this day.

I was called in to meet with the Continental Congress today—I had been all but promised a major generalship after all that I have done for this country in these times of revolutionary war. I expected to be granted the official word when I arrived, but was instead met with a different outcome.

It seems the Continental Congress does not approve of this blog. Of my personal thoughts about the war and how it's being handled. That I have recounted many stories about myself and my good friend <u>General George Washington</u>. Without even giving me a chance to remove this blog from circulation, they instead chose to deny me this position and any other future positions because of my writing. Sure, they offered me a position to serve under General Horatio Gates—but it is clearly an insult.

That the Continental Congress sees fit to deny a true leader a position such as this in a time where they need strong, dedicated and intelligent commanders makes me question just exactly the intelligence of this government. That they should deny ME brings me to the conclusion that my services are being substantially undervalued.

Perhaps there is some other group of individuals who might better appreciate my knowledge and the amount of intelligence I currently possess. Perhaps that is the next step in my life. Perhaps.

Will I continue this blog now that I have been punished for writing it? Yes.
Will I continue this blog now that I have been reprimanded for it? Yes.
Will I continue to share my thoughts and insights into how many holes there currently are in the American military plan? Indeed, I will.

While I try to shake this from my mind, please feel free to read previous entries such as: <u>How the British Could Beat the Americans, Pt 1 & 2</u>, <u>Boston's Weakness by Sea</u>, and <u>If I Were a Prisoner of the British Monarchy, Here's What I'd Tell Them</u>.

Good reading.

If anyone knows of other opportunities I might be interested in, please e-mail me.

From: **http://www.socrates.gr/blog/**

Subject: **What Is a Subject?**

What is a good subject?

What should I write here? What words would you want to see? What words could I place here that would keep you coming back for more discourse? Do I have the courage or motivation to make such ideas a reality?

What knowledge do the answers to those questions give you? Do you know less than you knew before you read them? Do you, indeed, know nothing about anything?

What should I write here?

Should I write something you want to read? Or, in fact, if I wrote something that you wanted to read, would you want to read it any longer? If I wrote something that you didn't want to read, would you want to read it more?

Are you still reading? Why are you still reading?

If you are reading to learn more, why do you want to learn more? And if you want to learn more simply to be more learned, then why do you want to be more learned? Is this something that will give you virtue? Courage? What is virtue? What is courage?

Why am I asking you these questions?

Do you think I am asking you these questions to find the answers? Or am I asking these questions to find out what are not the answers? Do you want to know the answers? If you do, why do you feel the need to know everything? And if you feel as though knowing everything makes you complete, why do you feel the need to be complete?

Should this entry be complete? Or should it simply end without w—

Did you see what I did there? I pretended like I was going to end the post but I didn't. How did that make you feel? Did you feel as though you were cheated? Did that make you mad? If so, why did that make you mad? And if it made you mad because you don't like being cheated, why is that?

You can give me your answers <u>here</u>.

(There are 6,542 more questions available for you to answer <u>here</u> (Pt 1) and <u>here</u> (Pt 2).

From: **http://www.edwardjohnsmith.com/shipslog/**

Subject: **Retirement!**

It's finally here—my last voyage as Captain of a vessel before I retire and leave the high seas behind. As you most likely are aware, I will be at the helm for the maiden voyage of the RMS *Titanic*—which will leave England on April 10 on its way to New York City.

I am so excited!!! This is going to be so much fun!

Yesterday evening, my friends and family gathered to see me off on this major milestone and wouldn't you guess—they made up a simply <u>embarrassing shirt</u> for me to wear in my off-hours. An obvious joke, and referencing the time while I was captaining the *Germanic* in 1899 when my ship capsized due to ice accumulations—they handed me a shirt with what appears to be a huge iceberg on it. I tried it on and we laughed for hours at how obscure such a situation was! Once in a lifetime, I guess.

Some of our family friends crafted a song that was simply inspired—it was called Edward "Full Speed Ahead" Smith and made fun of the time when I was in charge of the *Olympic*—when it was damaged during a collision with another ship named the HMS *Hawke*. It was lyrically humorous and sung to the tune of "Old McDonald":

Edward John Smith had a ship,
Uh oh, oh my God.
And on that ship, he had some people,
Uh oh, oh my God.
With a boom crash here,
And a crash boom there,
Here a leak, there a leak, everywhere a wet leak!
Edward John Smith crashed his ship,
Uh oh, oh my God!

Haha—they are so funny. You can hear us singing the song <u>here</u>.

As always, when the night ended, and all the jokes about my previous accidents were left behind as silly little memories—we all shared a moment and they wished me well. It was, to say the least, a wonderful evening before this monumental journey I am about to undertake.

Fortunately, retirement will be here before I know it. I can't wait!!

From: **http://www.darwin.com/blog/**

Subject: **The Mother-in-Law**

All God-fearing men find that there are some things more fearful than the wrath of the Almighty—which this poor soul found out two fortnights ago upon meeting for the first time my beloved's mother.

I must say, it being the first time, my stomach was tied and twisted . . . My skull headachy and clouded with questions. My health, which had been good up until that moment, was quick to fall. My dearest E's mother had a look about her that which I had never seen before.

My finger to put a point on it, after a longish evening of tea and crackers, the thought came to me. Respectful as I could be, I did not mention the thought to E until after we had left her mother behind. It was then that I said to E just what I was thinking. Her mother, however nice and motherly and helpful—her facial features (things I am quite aware of due to my work as a naturalist) reminded me of the African gorilla.

She was not pleased to say the least.

As I've said numerous times prior, my belief is that all creatures were created in the beginning . . . and remained as such throughout time. But in that moment, staring down the nose of my dearest wife's mother's face—I began to wonder if indeed such thoughts might be wrong. For, what if E's mother-in-law, of the human species, was at some point not human at all? Perhaps, the longest ancestor removed . . . of an animal species?

My beloved, of course, was cross with my thoughts and I apologized, for 'twas not meant to harm emotionally. But today, I cannot stop thinking about this idea. It is, yes, against God's original plan—but what if there is another explanation?

I received a letter last month from those planning a worldwide expedition on the HMS *Beagle*—looking for a naturalist on a trip to the strange Galápagos islands. I had disregarded such a trip for there was no reason for me to go—for what hypothesis would I be able to prove in such a place? That is, now, my thoughts betray me.

My mother-in-law looks like an ape. And I must find the reason for such a thing—and the one place I know where to look is, out there, in nature.

I have placed on here, <u>side by side</u>, a picture of my beloved's mother and the African gorilla. While I am gone, you may discuss amongst yourselves if you think my beliefs have merit or are simply the insane mutterings of a less-than-respectful husband.

From: **http://www.pt_barnum.com/blog/**

Subject: **Current Job Openings at Barnum Amusements!**

Most of you reading this blog are familiar with the famous midget "General Tom Thumb" and the famous show which I produced with him. We have had a rollicking run but now it is time for new performers to take his place! We are currently hiring new performers!!

Please <u>e-mail me</u> if you have any of the following talents and/or deformities . . . or you know someone who does. You can also upload your résumé <u>here</u> or create one in the <u>Barnum Résumé-a-Popper</u>!

Barnum Amusements Is Currently Looking For:

- Women who look like men.
- Men who look like women who look like men.
- Midgets who fancy eating a ton of cheese.
- Native Americans who have piercings and dance exotically.
- People who can squirt liquid out of their nose or ears.
- Extremely tall or fat people who have squeaky voices.
- Half-animal/half-humans.
- People who are missing limbs and/or have deformities who are comfortable working with squirrels.
- Ugly fat babies that are cross-eyed.
- Double-jointed foreigners with strange accents.
- Really scary, ugly people.

Barnum Amusements Is Also Looking for People Who Can Fit These Performer Titles:

- The Regurgitator
- The Milkman
- The Alcoholic Mouseman

- Zalmach the Attractor
- Miniature Mel
- The Newspaper Delivery Boy
- Hammerhead Hal
- Mexican Magician
- Two-Timing Flipper Baby
- The Astounding Dirt Licker
- Egg-Laying Lola
- The Blowhard
- The Earless Wonder
- Unnamed Strange-Lookin' Fella (this name is subject to change)

From: **http://www.dante_alighieri.com/blog/**

Subject: **Hell! Can Now Be Yours!**

ABANDON ALL HOPE!
HELL IS HERE!

(Now Available for <u>Download</u>!)

Unbaptized Pagans!
Gluttons!
Sloths!
Heretics!
Seducers!
Flatterers!
Rivers of Blood!
Hypocrites!
Thieves!
Traitors!
Disease!

The Circles of HELL can now be yours to own!

(Disclaimer: The author is not directly responsible for providing said "circles of Hell" to the purchaser upon checkout. Such "circles of Hell" are not located in the physical universe and cannot be guaranteed to materialize upon completing the transaction. Author does, however, guarantee that if said customer can aspire to each of the above Hell-like categories referenced above, they can be 99% sure that upon leaving the material world they will indeed visit said "circles of Hell.")

No refunds or credits. No guarantees.
Hell may not be as hellish as previously suggested.
Hell may not be engulfed in flames.
"Owning Hell" is a play on words.
"99%" may, in actuality, be closer to 11%.

From: **http://www.maewest.com/sex_blog/**

Subject: **For My Male Fans . . .**

You know what I always say, boys—a hard man is good to find! So why not contribute to making more boys bad?

My official <u>webcam</u> is now up and running . . . for your pleasure and mine. And from the hits so far, all I can tell you is that there are so many men and so little time to, well, do something with them all. I hope you enjoy it—all of me, for all of you! (As for my female fans—I hope you enjoy it just as much if not more than the boys!)

Thanks to all who have written letters in support of me after I was arrested while performing my off-Broadway play *Sex*. By now you probably know that the police shoved me into a jail cell for ten days . . . But I got out in eight days. Two days early for good behavior they say.

Good behavior, huh? Try bad behavior. Being a bad girl is what got me outta the slammer so quick. Those lonely guards. Stuck all day guarding bad criminals. I showed them a really really bad girl and it made their day. I woulda stayed ten more days if they'd let me, but you can imagine no one was gettin' any work done!

Since I've been back, I've been writin' another show. I ain't quite sure what the exact story's gonna be about, but I know for sure that I want it to include the following elements:

Sex

Have you checked out my <u>pictures</u> yet? This week I uploaded pictures of yours truly at the beach, playing cricket (you'll see how it's really done) and a little bit of strip poker with some of the boys down at the ol' watering hole. Strip poker's gotta be my favorite game 'cause when you lose . . . you really win!

I'll be back tomorrow with details of my night out with two men at once! Double the pleasure . . . for them, of course.

From: **http://www.joseph_mccarthy.com/blog/**

Subject: **Speaking Out Against the Offenders**

The problem has reached a critical point in our nation. All across this country, the offenders laugh in the face of what is right and what is just. As senator, in addition to my other successful missions, I have decided to take on yet another in an attempt to serve my country as they elected me to do.

It's about time someone took on these bloggers who refuse to put a picture of themselves on their blogs. And that someone is me.

 ← That's me.

In a time where alliances to this country are questioned at every corner, where Communists can be found in PTA meetings and the workplace—hiding and plotting . . . Isn't it time that all dishonest individuals be brought to justice?

If you have a blog and you do not have a picture of yourself on that blog—you are lying to the American public. You are hiding who you are. You are keeping secrets from those who look for information in a public forum. You must be stopped.

Therefore, I have decided that it will be my job to confront each and every blogger who erects their own blog and affixes them with images of animals, patterns, icons, colors, pictures heavily changed in graphic editing programs, and/or no images at all. If you are a person, with an honest agenda, then your face should be seen.

Isn't it ironic, that those without pictures often combine their lack of identity with potentially subliminal messages layered into dated MIDI songs in the code of their pages? Isn't it suspicious that those without pictures often talk more emphatically about the political system and how it refuses to work for their anonymous selves? Isn't it amusing that those without pictures also mis-direct e-mails to mailboxes that cannot be traced back to who they are?

The practice must stop. And I will be sure that it happens.

If you know anyone—friends, family, co-workers or siblings—who is currently using a blog or webpage and has not included an honest representation of who they are, you can send me an anonymous tip and my office will investigate them in due time.

We will address these issues along with finding a way to deal with those who post pictures from their vacations or provide links to photo albums that no one has previously expressed interest in. Such practices are obviously a cover—a way to force one's negative ideals onto other innocent Americans.

Fight with me! E-mail me.

From: http://www.blogger.com/~louis_pasteur/

Subject: • • •

Qwertyuiop[]\ASDFGHJKL;"
Zxcvbnm,./

Excuse me—it was necessary to clean off the keyboard prior to using it.

`1234567890-=

Sorry, didn't get the top layer of the keyboard.

So, the discussion yesterday centered around how spores attach themselves to dust and enter our households, thus infecting our lives with germs. I originally had a diagram which I had readied for this site, but unfortunately it become contaminated by the canine, and had to obviously be burned immediately.

Rrrrrrrrrrrrrrrrrrrrrrrrrrrrrrrrrrrrrrrrrrrrrrrrrrrrrrrrrrrr

Again, I apologize. The "r" key had more than its share of dirt caked onto the top layer of its surface. Using a cleansing agent I believe I'm now working with a fully sanitized keyboard.

I've received quite a lot of correspondence lately from those of you as concerned as I am about keeping the devices we use to communicate as free of germs as possible. In doing so, I would like to provide you with this <u>link</u> to a blank white page. This will allow you to see if there is any offending dirt or dust invisibly hiding from your human eyes. Of course, spores are too small for the human eye and so the only way in which to determine if your workspace is cluttered by such evil particles is to take the following steps:

1. Cover your entire device in an oversized plastic bag.
2. Secure a filter at the end of said oversized plastic bag.
3. Suck air from the plastic bag, through the filter.
4. Examine the filter.

If said filter is filled with spores (which you will need a microscope of some kind to determine), then your computer has been affected by dust spores. Such spores may or may not be noxious, but in order to be safe you should do what I always do . . . Assume the worst. Dispose of the computer immediately.

Germs are everyyyyyyyyyyyyyyyyyyyyyyyyy (sorry, "y" key was still dirty) . . . are everywhere.

From: **http://www.harryhoudini.com/blog/**
Subject: **Happened Again!**

I was on the way home tonight with my wife, Bess, from yet another one of my bird shows. Yes, "The King of Birds" show, once again, brought down the house. Bess, as always, did a wonderful job as my assistant . . . always on her toes, as my trademark "doves vanish in midair" is a tricky one to handle (that's all I can say, don't want to give away any of the secrets!).

At around sundown, we arrived home to find that we were (once again) locked out of the house.

Bess always ribs me about this, and didn't let up tonight with her *this is the fifteenth time you have forgotten the keys, Ehrich* spiel, and no matter what I tried (jiggling the lock, kicking it with my foot, trying to loosen the hinges)—there was no giving. No solution.

It was mildly comical if you picture the situation. Me in my stage costume, Bess in hers. Cages of birds stacked by the dozens. A dark night sky. And there we were, for (yes, it's true) the fifteenth time . . . locked out of our home.

After calling the locksmith we eventually found our way in (would I be writing this sad little entry now if that wasn't the case?) and settled in at a much later time than we had previously expected. The whole experience has got me thinking, of course, that maybe the life of a locksmith isn't that bad. In a way, it's somewhat magical, the way the tumblers and the locks work in unison to unlock a door. The way one man, with just his hands, can free the bonds of any steel structure.

Quite astounding if you ask me. I could have watched the locksmith for hours—yet for him, it only required a mere thirty seconds.

Fast and amazing. Life's true magician!

From: **http://www.polofamily.com/~marco/**

Subject: **Lost in China**

Hello, again!

Last week I spoke about the greatest honor in all of my journey thus far, with Father and Uncle Maffeo, when the Kublai Khan made me his official emissary for when we return to Rome. In the meantime, I have detailed some of the amazing cultural differences of China, from their chopsticks (two staffs of wood, for eating!), the amazing Great Wall, and my favorite by far—the tea. No tea tastes better on the tongue, as you will all experience when my family returns to Venice where we shall share our discoveries.

A funny and harrowing story to share:

A few nights ago my father, Niccolo, was invited to a meal hosted by the Khan—and instructed to bring his brother and son to the festivities. We were happy, as usual, to attend, as it provided us the opportunity to continue to learn and experience the culture here in China.

After a wonderful dinner, I excused myself to explore the elaborate gardens out behind the palace—twisting branches and flowers, rising high above my head and forming walls on all sides. They twist and turn like two snakes intertwined, yet I made my way further into them, as my mind was not concerned with where I was, but what I saw. You can imagine my surprise when I found myself lost. I tried, of course, to find my way, but was met with impasses at every corner. Eventually, of course, I sat down and waited. And waited. And waited. Then suddenly I heard:

"Marco!?"

The voice echoed throughout the night sky—it was, of course, Uncle Maffeo.

I yelled back, *" 'Tis I, Polo!"*

"Marco!?" the voice came back again, echoing . . .

"Polo!" I yelled. Could he not hear me?

"Marco!!!" my uncle yelled again, this time seemingly closer.

"Here!" I yelled. *"Polo!!!"*

The two of us might as well have been in a dark cave or the murky underwater depths of the ocean for that matter—blind to each other's face, the simple yelling of our names never close to providing the solution.

This must have gone on until the morning light, when Maffeo asked for assistance in which to navigate the guarded pathways and finally located me.

It was, to say the least, a less than entertaining event that I would never wish upon any individual, young or old.

From: **http://www.wcfields.com/blog/**

The Official W. C. Fields Weblog

YOU MUST BE 18 OR OLDER TO ENTER

ENTER   EXIT

(Seriously, no kids.)
(Not even with your parents' permission.)

(I mean it.)

From: **http://www.johnhancock.com/blog/**

Subject: **Today's Official Declaration**

A milestone in the history of these United States of America . . . today, as had been planned for some time now, our Declaration of Independence, drafted and signed by a select group of patriots and statesmen. Yours truly was honored to be among them.

You can't imagine the feelings of inspiration that floated throughout Independence Hall today, standing beside such friends and countrymen as Thomas Jefferson (he's drafted quite a <u>wonderful poem</u> on his site from today) and Benjamin Franklin (who has got <u>pictures</u> of the event in question up on his weblog).

I must share with you an amusing anecdote from the day's events, however—as all of us stood toe-to-toe, preparing to ink our names onto the document in question . . . Thomas leaned forward and picked up the inkwell and the pen, but when he went to inscribe his name on the document, he slipped and fell mid-signature! But Thomas, always quite dedicated to the cause at hand, attempted to finish his name before hitting the ground.

The result—a curved, grandiose signature that was the cause of laughter for the rest of the lively scenario! And as each statesman reached the table and the document, those who had already signed began to chant, *"Give us your Thomas Jefferson!"* in reference, of course, to his elaborate penned signature!

"Give us your Thomas Jefferson!" Even now, it causes me to smile a silly grin—a situational joke that, I'm sure, will stick with these men and History for years to come.

While the day was a milestone none of us will soon forget, I find my thoughts turning toward my own last name, the cruelty of children and the phrase "John the cock"—the subject of many years of despair on my part, that even today (after such a monumentally historic moment) brings chills to my spine. I can only hope, that years from now when fresh eyes gaze upon this Declaration, the jokes of days gone by are no more than memories . . .

That would make both me and my mother a pair of happy Hancocks, proud in name and reputation.

Don't miss my <u>pictures from today</u>—you'll especially want to check out <u>this one</u> with Jefferson landing on his backside and tumbling to the ground! Hoo-wee!

From: **http://www.marktwain.com/blog/**

Subject: **"The Paying Kind" and Other Stories . . .**

'Twas the kind of day when a man would far prefer the scent of the summer air all by its lonesome rather than the background for a far less appealing chore.

If I've said it once I'll say it once again—I have never been the kind of man who connects with the ones and the zeroes. I have never been the kind of soul who can stare for hours into the blank canvas of a digital screen. And above all, while I fancy myself an artist, I can never design a digital version of what you're now gazing upon.

Which brings me back to the kind of day I mentioned prior—'twas my chore for the day, sitting there in the open air on my front porch, attempting to design what you are now lookin' at. But at the time, I slaved over something that wasn't coming.

My neighbor approached around noontime, curiously looking upon what I was slaving over. *"Good day,"* he said. *"Whatchya got there?"*

Well, my smarts got the better of my brain at the moment, and before I spoke I took the time to place my words in a careful order. *"What am I doing?"* I spoke with excitement . . . *"Most probably the most amusing, fun, rewarding thing any man on a sunny day like today could do! Designing my brand-new digital scribble sheet!"*

My neighbor looked at me with jealousy as I turned back to the screen, poking and tapping away with a whistle from my mouth. He leaned in closer, curiously. *"Do you think maybe I could help ya?"* he wondered.

"Oh, no no no no no," I replied. *"This is important business that I can't just hand over to anyone. Besides, why would I let someone else do something that I enjoy as much as I do? I'd be crazy to just step aside and let someone have all the fun!"*

My neighbor stood quiet for a moment, tongue hangin' out the side of his mouth. Then his eyes lit up like a candle's flame and he dug deep into his pocket. My neighbor turned to me, leaned in close and spoke, *"I'll pay you if you'll let me."*

I looked to him with eyebrows raised. *"You want to pay me so you can take over the design?"* I asked. *"You're asking me to step aside and let you do the whole business?"* He nodded affirmatively as he pulled a wad of money from his pocket, shoving it into my palm.

By the time the sun was hangin' close to the horizon, my pockets were filled with green. My neighbor, his cousin and four more locals had heard of the exciting activity at the Twain estate that would only cost them a day's work!

Sometimes, perception, it seems, is far more appealing than conception. Of which, this site has now experienced thanks to some very passionate, very gullible locals!

From: **http://www.howardhughes.com/blog/**

Subject: **The Benefits of Keeping Urine in a Jar**

Urine.

Urine urine urine urine urine.

Doesn't sound like a real word anymore when you say it twenty-one times.

Urine Urine.

What is urine? What is it? What is it what is it what is it? It's urine. Urine Urine Urine Urine Urine Urine Urine Urine Urine Urine Urine Urine Urine Urine Urine Urine Urine.

I wrote about urine. Twenty-one times before. You can read those entries [here], [here], [here], [here], [here], [here], [here], [here], [here], [here], [here], [here], [here], [here], [here], [here], [here], [here], [here], [here] and [here]. I also wrote about peas. I like peas, and that's a word I can stand behind! Peas. Please. Peas. Please. Please, peas.

People are talking about me. Me. Me. Me. Me. Me. No, I do not wear tissue boxes for shoes. No, I am not dead. No, these rumors are the creations of governments who seek to destroy me. Me and my urine! Urine.

Yes, I keep my urine in a jar. It is sanitary. Sanitary. Sanitary. Tell me about what's not sanitary and I'll tell you what is sanitary. And while I'm telling you what is sanitary you'll have to excuse me while I fill up a jar with my urine. Urine.

Yes, it's a word. Urine is. But it's not nearly the kind of word that peas is. Peas is a word you can stand behind. I wouldn't be caught dead standing behind, above or in such a word as urine.

It's fun running a huge corporation funded by millions of dollars in capital.

. . . . Twenty-one dots. There are twenty-one dots there. This is my new signature. This is a much safer signature. One that cannot be forged. People are out to get me and my jars and my peas and I must be ingenious to outwit them.

More later!

From: **http://www.isaacnewton.com/blogstore/**

Subject: **On the Subject of Gravitation (and, Shirts)**

'Tis the subject of gravitation that has most likely drawn you, dear readers, to my location here. And wherest I initially found it confounding that such subject matter would resonate so deeply with the public, time told the tale and proved me wrong.

Soon after, the letters began arriving—many from those who once knew me at Cambridge and continue to make my acquaintance to this day. Others, looking for the "Newton Apple"—that which struck me upon my head which sparked the notion of gravitation into my mind. Before long, the tale of the Newton Apple shirt was born!

Just as the famous "Newton apple" descended downward (and not sideways or upward) due to gravity—so too has the price of the Newton Apple Shirt (pictured below)!

(Newton Apple Shirt in S, M, L, XL, XXL)

Made from the finest wool from the finest sheep from the finest county around (Lincolnshire), the "Newton Apple Shirt" can be worn with your finest threads, to events big and small, all the while you will subtly be communicating your belief in gravity, your support of yours truly, and your love of all apples great and small.

[Click here to purchase!]

Other "Newton Apple" products are well on their way! The "Newton Apple Tunic," the "Newton Apple Wig" and the most widely requested item since the inception of this site, the "Newton Apple, Apple"!

From: **http://www.alanturing.com/blog/**
Subject: **011000011001**

0010011100111100101000100110011001100110011100010101001001100100100100100111
0011000011010101001001100110011001001001001000011010101010100010101000100100 01.

0010011100111100101000100110011001100110011100010101001001100100100100100111
0011000011010101001001100110011001001001000011010101010100010101000100001001
1100111100101000100110011001100110011100010101001001100100100100100111001100
0011010101001001100110011001001001001000011010101010100010101000100.

0010011100111100101000100110011001100110011100010101001001100100100100100111
0011000011010101001001100110011001001001001000011010101010100010101000100011000
0110101010010011001100110010010010010000110101010101000101010001000010011100111
1001010001001100110011001100111000101010010011001001001001001001110011000011010
10100100110011001100100100100100001101010101010001010100010 0!!

0010011100111100101000100110011001100110011100010101001001100100100100100111
0011000011010101001001100110011001001001001000011010101010100010101000100.

0010011100111100101000100110011001100110011100010101001001100100100100100111
0011000011010101001001100110011001001001001000011010101010100010101000100001001
1100111100101000100110011001100110011100010101001001100100100100100111001100
0011010101001001100110011001001001001000011010101010100010101000100 . . .
0010011100111100101000100110011001100110011100010101001001100100100100100111
0011000011010101001001100110011001001001001000011010101010100010101000100.

0010011100111100101000100110011001100110011100010101001001100100100100100111
0011000011010101001001100110011001001001001000011010101010100010101000100.

0101010101010000011010100100101010001001001000001010101010100010101010000 1010
10100001110010101001010.

01010001110.

From: **http://www.pocahontas-theAlgonquian.com/blog/**

Subject: **Powhatan, Kocoum and I**

First, please forgive me and my URL. It became apparent to me, however horribly, that another Algonquian from Tenakomakah swooped in like an eagle and took the pocahontas.com domain name. It appears as if there are more than one of our tribe who consider themselves "playful" and "frolicsome" and deserving of a place to express their thoughts.

If you have come looking for Matoaka (Pocahontas), then you are in the correct place. If you are looking for the other who calls herself Shurbaota (Pocahontas), then you should turn around and go <u>here</u>.

Now to Powhatan and Kocoum.

My father, whom you all know (Powhatan), has seen fit to determine who it is that I, a young girl of only twelve seasons, should join with. This . . . Kocoum. At first, all that I could muster was a growl of a tiger . . . The annoying screech of the midnight owl. The quiet of the reeds in the Tenakomakah waters was nowhere to be heard. I was angered, but could not do anything against my father.

Shaori and I sat and talked for some time about being promised to another. She, of course, gave my soul a great deal of peace when she suggested that at least we weren't being forced on the white man. The colonists who come from far away, eating up the land like carnivores. We laughed about the horrid white man and their technologies. Their dirtiness. Their inability to communicate. Their lack of respect for the nature that surrounds us all.

At least you don't have to be with a white man, Shaori told me. It was a truth as real as the grass beneath our bare feet.

When my father placed me alongside Kocoum, as he stripped the carcass of a doe, I found myself humbled by his strength and courage and honor and dedication to both my father, our tribe and me. And he wasn't a white man. Eiiiiwwwwwwww. Gross.

The lesser of two evils is always the best in any decision . . .

And so, I, Matoaka—will look forward to the time when my age will ripen and to when Kocoum and I will find our paths intertwined . . . Together . . . Fate will find us, as it always does!

Check <u>him out</u>! Look at his bare, rocklike stomach!

From: **http://www.hgwells.com/**

Subject: **Queries Abound!**

Indeed, it's no surprise I'm still attempting to complete my latest novel, one which looks as if it will be the first published document ever in my life—an honor that I must admit both frightens me and inspires me. Nonetheless, I have yet to explain the concept but I must keep it a secret until the final version of the book has been unveiled.

Yes, I will admit that the novel is taking much longer than previously expected—but it is not due to any creative block of the mind, of that you must be sure. I simply must get things perfect. This is my goal. I have received many letters from those wondering when this delayed manuscript will be forthcoming (including my publishers) but there is nothing to fear. This first book will be completed extremely soon! All of the hard questions have been answered—I am simply dotting my i's and crossing my t's and putting the very very final final touches on my masterpiece!

In the meantime, in an attempt to keep my audience constantly guessing, I am putting up a brand-new feature I have dubbed "Questions from Beyond" where you answer questions you have absolutely no real basis of study in answering, but which you answer nonetheless, simply because I ask you to. (Again, these are random hypothetical questions, in no particular order, whose subject matter really has nothing to do with anything.)

Question #1: Let's say you created a machine that would allow you to travel through time. Where would you go?

Question #2: Assume for a second that something like that was even possible (which it's not, and no one is even postulating or writing about such a fact), but once you got there, what do you think you'd find?

Question #3: Do you think you'd be pleased if you met a female of the species there? Would she have light hair or dark hair? Would she wear clothing that accentuated her legs?

Question #4: On a totally unrelated note, would you call this machine simply "the time machine" or would you name it after a family member (e.g., the HG Wells Machine)?

Question #5: Changing subjects for a moment—if you had to name a strange group of people you'd never met before in a strange society you'd never been to before some fashion of strange foreign-sounding name, what name do you think you'd use?

Question #6: Totally going off subject again, but I must wonder aloud—would a story about a machine going into another time benefit from adding in political commentary or allegorical references to today's society?

Question #7: Do you fancy fish and chips? Or tea and crumpets?

Yes, I know. Simply ludicrous notions and questions just for the sake of asking silly little questions of my readers! Sometimes, the stranger and more nonsensical questions make this feature even more amusing! I can't wait to see your responses when you send them to me at hgwells@wells.co.uk. Seriously, send them soon so I can laugh about them with my colleagues! Send them now, if you can. I have to go out later and I'd like to read them all very quickly before I have to go out . . . I have dinner with my publisher! Yes, just answer them now. Go ahead. Do it now.

If you can send some of your answers tonight, I'll take time out from finishing my first novel to peruse your simply crazy answers to such illogical queries.

As for the book . . . the finished copy will be completed very very very soon!

Thank you!

HG.

From: **http://www.odysseus.gr/blog/**

Subject: **Helen = Problems**

May Zeus save me from this curse!

You may remember my <u>previous entry</u> about Helen, daughter of Tyndareus. The numerous suitors competing for her attention and hand in marriage. The final result being Menelaus. The suitors' agreement to defend Helen's choice in any future battles. And so on and so on and so on.

And now here I sit, years into the battle against the city of Troy—the result of Paris and Helen's forbidden love and him taking her from her rightful mate. The result of being recruited by Agamemnon (agamemmy@sparta.com) to defend her honor and return her home.

I am charged with filling a wooden device filled with soldiers that Epeius has been directed to build. The evening prior, while camped on the hill overlooking Troy, we discussed what sort of wooden device would fitfully hold enough warriors to do irreparable damage to the unsuspecting city of Troy.

Epeius drew up plans to build a boar, an ox, a cow and a rabbit. I looked over such plans but there appeared to be little space for those chosen to take on such a mission. I thought long and hard about size, the element of surprise, and the ease of skill in building such a device and came up with the final thought that . . .

. . . such a device is insanity.

Personally, had I woken up to a knock on the door of my estate and stood eye-to-eye with a lumbering, huge monolith in the shape of an ox or a cow or a boar . . . Suspicion would run rampant. Such creatures are simply not indigenous to these lands. Whoever's idea was such, should honestly be hung. Puh-leeeeze. A huge wooden animal? It'll never work!

I came up with an elephant! If you're going to build something . . . If you must build something, as it has been ordered, then the least suspicious of all in the kingdom of animals is the elephant! Of this I am sure. Elephants, I have heard, at least will travel from door to door in a populated area or throughout the countryside. They are sociable animals that I think would not shy away from a quick greeting or knock at the door. But an ox or a cow or a boar or a rabbit? Not sociable animals at all, nor do they have a trunk, which is perfect for knocking on things. An elephant. That is what it must be.

I will present this idea when morrow comes—as for this evening, I will practice my reasons for building such a nonsuspicious creature out of wood.

May Zeus protect my ideas from being ignored!

From: **http://www.london_jack.com/ripper-blog/**

Subject: **Another Lonely Night . . .**

Aaah, another lonely night as the words prior so eloquently state.

Here I sit, with my feet up by the fireplace, hot cup of tea by my side . . . Both my little best friends lying at my feet (Willingsworth and Frannie, the English setters) . . . And a wish in my heart for a soul mate just like myself.

The luck, it seems, is only set aside for the Irish and not the English, as I am.

Often I sit, scribbling in my journal, writing about the future I see for myself. A loving wife, whom I adore and wait on hand and foot—bringing her flowers for simple occasions and rubbing her feet after a hard day's labour. The two of us, we're inseparable. We finish each other's sentences. She adores me almost as much as I adore her. How can there be no woman who matches such qualities in a city as large as London?

Sometimes, I find myself walking the night streets looking for such a soul mate. Looking for a woman who makes my life complete. Fills my face with colour. Completes my soul in a way that turns its half into a whole.

But alas, she [or you, if you are reading this] is never there.

I am a respectful man. A successful man. A dedicated man. My looks, they may not slay a thousand maids but they are not off-putting. But beauty, at least in my eyes, is never just on the surface. It's what's inside that matters most. As such, when I meet a lady for the first time, I do not gaze endlessly at her milky white skin or her supple breasts—but I instead gaze deep into her eyes and into her soul. That is where a true woman exists.

Did I mention my e-mail? You can get me a message at jack@londonjack.com.

Sadly, no one has contacted me via such a way, but I am always hopeful that someday the woman I am fated to meet will contact me. That the two of us will meet in a neutral place, preferably late at night (I am truly a night owl, when the stars are bright in the night sky and the fog has lifted) and that she will fall for me in a way she has never fell before.

Here's to you milady—wherever you are!

J.

From: http://www.thomas_crapper.com/blog/
Subject: Another Visit with Your Favorite Crapper!

I spent some valuable time with the littlest Crapper in all of England this past weekend when I was invited to the Norfolk house of Prince Edward to consult him about adding an astounding thirty lavatories to his Sandringham House.

George, my nephew, who is indeed the smallest Crapper in the entire family, was invited to the job so that he may learn the ins and outs of being a well-respected, highly admired, thorough and professional Crapper. Needless to say, the little Crapper has got a lot to learn if he ever wants to match up to the biggest Crappers in the family business.

Upon returning home, I finished the item pictured here, that I have previously mentioned to you through this blog, that I have called the "ballcock"—a floating mechanism I believe will someday make my "valveless water waste preventer" a reality. Personally, I must say that there's nothing more exciting than being a bona fide Crapper and holding a ballcock in your hands at the same time. Just knowing that this family of Crappers was responsible is more than worthwhile.

As you've all seen in the advertisements, we Crappers want to bring a comfortable and sanitary experience to you and to a lavatory that will serve as an extension to your main house. As a well-known Crapper, you know that such a thing is the highest on my list of priorities.

But before presenting people with my ballcock, integrated into a toilet, it is necessary to come up with a variety of names for this new device that would honor some of the greatest Crappers around. Such a name should be dignified and instill respect and when the time is right, I will reveal the chosen phrase to all. The official name for one of civilization's most civilized devices! Here's a couple of such ideas to whet your appetite:

- Underground water-filled pipe mechanism
- Force-powered lavatory symphonic flush
- Ceramic gold-plated sanitary sitting facility

My hope, of course, is that one of these very descriptive and honourable names will both describe the technology and honour yours truly as the dignified Crapper that I am . . . Doing my part in bringing comfort, safety and a solitude to those looking for the kind of experience that only a true Crapper can know.

<u>Pictures</u> of Sandringham House
<u>Pictures</u> of "My Ballcock"
<u>Pictures</u> of a Crapper, doing what he does best

E-mail me at <u>Crap4Thomas@crapper.com</u>.

From: **http://www.robertfrost.com/blog/**
Subject: **From New Hampshire to New York**

As I previously mentioned, I felt it necessary to take a trip for the soul this week. A journey from my home in New Hampshire to New York. Of course, the originating locale and the destination were never the important elements of such a journey—it's what's in between that matters.

Of course, without the luck of the Irish, I found myself halfway through my journey in a wooded place when a tire burst loudly and stranded me (a stranger in a strange land) with no map, no directions, and a winding road becoming two. My direction, of course, was as lost to me as I was lost myself.

One, it seemed, had been traveled on repeatedly. It was worn and weathered, traveled upon constantly on a daily basis, while another was overgrown, obviously avoided by many. With a flat tire and night rapidly approaching, I did what any sane man would do. I headed down the pathway, tire in hand, that was obviously traveled upon most frequently.

About three miles ahead, I found a gas station attendant who repaired my tire and gave me a ride back to my car where he assisted me in affixing the tire back onto the vehicle.

It was, to say the least, the best decision of my entire life.

Now, back here in my study in beautiful and lush Franconia, I find myself searching for the rhythm and prose for my next poetic work. If only there was something in a flat tire and a walk to an out-of-the-way gas station . . . well, if only! Passion and creativity, it seems, do not come when you call it. You must wait for inspiration and be surprised by it . . . I guess, just as a flat tire rears its ugly head as well.

In the meantime, I would like to introduce a brand-new feature on my blog called <u>You Give Me a Dollar and I Write You a Poem with Your Name in It!</u> What better way to surprise your family or friends than a poem written about them, with their name included inside? Well, far better than a tie or a doll, I can tell you that.

This week only, if you enter this <u>code</u> while ordering, you'll be able to get three poems featuring someone's name for the price of two. That's a 33% discount!

Click <u>here</u> for ordering information.
Click <u>here</u> for sample poems.
Click <u>here</u> to e-mail Robert Frost.

From: **http://www.arthurconandoyle.com/blog/**

Subject: **The Case of the Missing Post**

The night is the darkest right at this moment, as I fill in this page with words that were once not needed . . . eclipsed by a post both ingenious and mysterious. A post filled with action, intrigue and drama. A post that, with an accidental flip of a button, went missing from wherest it once was. Such a post, one I crafted for hours, has now gone accidentally missing.

You can imagine my chagrin as the events unfolded. Quietly crafting, word by word, extremely pleased with the outcome and ready to send to the world when, all at once, the light went dark and the world on the page went missing completely.

My dear readers—you must know that at first I deduced that such an accidental happening was not the result of pure chance but one which was motivated by others who are less than pleased with my own success. I traipsed out into the darkness, finding none other than footprints measured in the snow. Such footprints led away from an electrical box beside my home to the road that stood 100 meters away. The shoe prints moved steadily and quickly, as the impression in the snow was still crisp and clean with no sign of melting or destruction. My observation seemed astute until I came face-to-face with my neighbour who had also been searching for the reason behind such an electrical mystery.

So, then, what was the cause of the missing post? For what reason would a document I had created suddenly disappear to origins unknown? I searched high and low around my sitting area—tracing the cord of the device down to the floor. The wood panels, aged from the years, had a dusty film upon them. Although, upon further investigation, it was apparent that such dust had shaken from the sides of my socks—sitting in shoes that had seen the outdoors.

And so I looked even further below my space—crawling in a place that my body was never meant to be. My deduction about foul play may be correct, I recall thinking to myself as I dug deeper, further into the darkness beneath my sitting area in an attempt to solve this mysterious case of the missing post.

And then, almost immediately, the mystery was solved! There, unplugged and lying dormant on the wood-paneled floor, was none other than the plug to my device. My foot it seems had pulled the device's power on its own accord, replacing any suspicion of foul play with the common solution in its place—pure human error.

Just know that whatever post was once here—it would have entertained you to the fullest. A short story of intrigue, mystery and malcontents. But alas, maybe this one will far surpass, seeing as though a mystery emerged and was solved right before your very own eyes! My breath, as much as yours, has most probably been taken away!

-CD

From: **http://www.samson.com/hairblog/**

Subject: **Another Inch in Gaza**

Some of you may already have received the "Official Samson Hair Status Subscription List" (you can subscribe <u>here</u> if not); then you are all well aware that my hair has grown another inch longer and I am feeling stronger than ever before. The <u>Samson Hair Length Photo Gallery</u> is now open for your perusal.

If you do not have the technology to view such pictures, let me take a moment to describe to you how my strength-filled hair now appears to a stranger who might glance upon it while walking down the street.

Imagine this—if you were to walk behind me, you would see my luscious locks hang effortlessly down to the edge of my neck where it meets my shoulders, then fall and lie over the tops of my shoulder muscles. Really, it's a sight to behold that you may want to see in person. I'm in Gaza right now, in case you are too.

Speaking of Gaza, it appears as if another woman has fallen in love with yours truly and his hair. Her name is Delilah, and I must say that this beauty has also found her way into my heart. We have spent some time together, but last night she appeared to be out of her element. She wrestled me to the ground, pinning my arms at the floor (which I could have broken out of thanks to the strength my hair gives me, but which I chose not to use at that moment because I was enjoying the interplay) and demanded to know the origin of my strength.

As you very well know, I try not to tell people that I'm strong because of my hair, because once you tell someone that—well, first they think you should probably be named a heretic and, second of all, they'll probably want to shave off your hair. (I mean, who doesn't want to own the hair that makes someone so exceptionally strong?! If I didn't own my own hair I would want to own my own hair if it was someone else's hair that they themselves owned.)

So, I told Delilah that my strength came from lifting heavy rocks and stones. Which she didn't believe. Then I told her that I was strong, just as my father was strong. And then I told her that it was the result of an angel's prophecy.

That Delilah is a pretty persuasive woman.

In the end, I told her the truth and let her in on the secret that the true strength I possess actually comes from my glorious locks of hair. And that without them, I am nothing. But since I trust her (she seems very honest), at least I know she won't tell anyone and that my secret is safe with her.

Besides, she said she promised not to tell a soul.

From: **http://www.jimjones.com/blog/**

Subject: **Kool-Aid or Hawaiian Punch?**

I can't quite decide which one I like better.

If you were planning a big ol' party with lots of friends, family members and relatives and you had to choose a particular punch because you were going to make that the center of the entire party/buffet—which one do you think would be more appealing?

Personally, I think Kool-Aid is the way to go. Kool-Aid seems to have a cheerier, happier mascot—the big happy glass bowl of Kool-Aid who comes crashing through people's walls screaming *"Oh yeah!"* Now, let's turn our attention toward Hawaiian Punch—their mascot is a strange-looking short individual who wears an awfully obscure hat on his head. As an adult or a child, I think I would personally much prefer the happy, energetic mascot used in the Kool-Aid ads to the creepy, short eerie-looking man.

But then again, people flock to Hawaii in the wintertime. Just thinking about the beaches and the waves of the Hawaiian coast puts me in a comfortable lull. It's paradise, Hawaii—all of the islands instill a calming effect in those who visit. So, perhaps in thinking about this new tidbit of information, Hawaiian Punch might be the better choice.

For example, if I were to turn to you and say, *"Would you like a glass of refreshing Kool-Aid, the drink whose mascot is a funny, happy little wall-crashing smiling jar of juice?"* or, *"Would you like a glass of paradise-like Hawaiian punch—the kind you'd probably end up drinking on a beautiful beach on the island of Maui?"* which question would urge you to swallow the liquid?

Now that I'm really thinking about it, I am starting to believe that Hawaiian Punch may be the way to go.

Then again, maybe the name recognition makes it seem as if I'm trying too hard to get people to drink the punch. Maybe if I were to simply pick up punch that wasn't well known, or make my own punch with fruit and juices straight off the vine—maybe that would seem more realistic. Maybe then, if I were to say, *"Would you like a glass of this wonderful punch which I have made from scratch from a variety of fruits I picked myself off the vine?"* . . . Maybe that would be the most realistic scenario.

Then again, I often don't eat or drink things that people make themselves because they're never really as good as the kind of fare you'd buy in a restaurant or in a grocery store.

Hmm. This is really a tough decision.

Kool-Aid or Hawaiian Punch? Be sure to send me your thoughts <u>here</u>. I look forward to hearing what you have to say in this important matter!

From: **http://www.raykroc.com/mcblog/**
Subject: **Welcome to Ray Kroc's McBlog**

The day has finally come!

I know we've been talking about this day for a while now and I am finally proud to announce that what you're reading here is the first official blog entry for the McBlog—a groundbreaking new addition to the McDonald's family that came out of a minor event in the Kroc family.

I was sitting with my children and we had just come back from a wonderful meal at our local McDonald's—we were eating fries and the wonderful Big Mac and a yummy vanilla shake when my son asked, *"Daddy—we can always get what we want, quickly and without wait, when we visit McDonald's, but how come we can't get the same quick, high-quality service when reading blogs?"*

And the McBlog was born.

From here on forward, the Ray Kroc McBlog will serve America's blogging needs twenty-four hours a day, three hundred and sixty-five days a year with blog posts that you want, when you want them, for a relatively low low price. Here's how it works:

Step #1: Feeling an urge to read a blog post? Login to the McBlog!
Step #2: From a pulldown menu, choose the subject matter you'd like to read about. Everything from humor, politics, food and games to pictures, music and the famous McDonald's characters themselves!
Step #3: Pay a small nominal fee, depending on your choice. Please note, on some days you'll be able to get two blog posts for the price of one . . . Other times you may be able to **expand** your blog post—instead of a 300-word post, you can turn it into a 500-word post for just 45 cents more!!
Step #4: Read your blog post until you're finished, at which point it will disappear. But if minutes later you're still feeling that desire for even more, we'll be here to serve you up another and another and another. There's no cap on how many you can read. It gets addicting, I know! When you stop is fully up to you!

But what makes the McBlog different from all other blogs? In a word . . . **usability**. Sick and tired of visiting a blog and not getting the same quality each and every time? Tired of showing up and not getting what you want? Fatigued by having to search long and hard for something to satisfy your inner self? Well, no longer.

As of the posting of this column, the McBlog is fully operational and available for your requests. We have some special deals coinciding with the launch today of the McBlog which we call our "Extra Value Posts"—just ask for the number that coincides with them and you'll be reading before you can say *Can I please have a blog post about dogs and how they look like their owners!*" Here's this week's extra value posts:

Extra Value Post #1: Two blog posts about any subject, an e-mail response from the author, and a small anecdote you can tell your friends over and over again at parties and social engagements. (Expand this offer for 45 cents and get a medium anecdote and a special edition haiku!)

Extra Value Post #2: One big post about politics or entertainment, a link to pictures that you can download for your desktop, and a link to an exclusive video file! (Expand this offer for 45 cents and get a post about the politics of entertainment.)

Extra Value Post #3: A post about fish. We don't expect this one to be as popular as all the rest, but we do believe that there's a market for blog posts about fish and so we're just gonna keep this one up here in case, you know, someone wants to read a post about fish. (Expand this offer for 45 cents and get, well, more stories about fish.)

Extra Value Kid's Post #4: A collection of posts without any indecent subject matter or bad language—this extra value kid's post also comes with a Flash-based game starring none other than the new McBlog mascot, the McBloggler. (Expand this offer for 45 cents and get an exclusive coupon for a Big Mac at one of our actual McDonald's restaurants!)

We hope this very special opening of the McBlog brings you and your family as much happiness as it's bringing the Kroc family. We think it's time that America doesn't have to search out the kind of blog they want—they should know exactly where it is. And where it is . . . is right here at the McBlog!

Thank you for visiting and your continuing patronage!

Ray Kroc

Hundreds and Hundreds of Entries Read

From: **http://www.drseuss.com/~blog/**

Subject: **The Things I Blog**

I blog at morning,
Midday and noon,
I blog with words,
I blog with tune.
I blog with humor,
I blog to please,
I've never blogged,
For a ton of cheese.

Gouda, cheddar, maybe Swiss,
I'd write and write, so I'd not miss,
A ton of cheese there on my plate,
I'd eat and eat, and then, I'd ate.

The things I blog are not for you,
And not for her, and not for Sue,
And not for James and not for Jen,
And definitely not for Sam the Hen.
The things I blog are every day,
Through February, March, April and May,
The things I blog come quick and fast,
Just so this place, it sure does last.

The things I blog are fun, it's true!
The things I blog are new, for you!
The things I blog are not for grumps,
Or icks or blechs or old tree stumps.

—Dr. Seuss

I hope you liked today's great rhyming post, I think out of the
week I love it the most. Did I mention that next week I'm flying
to the coast? Meeting up with friends for a huge big roast.

That doesn't mean the site will be dead. In fact, I hope to still post from my bed. Even if after the roast I feel like lead from all the drinks that went to my head! If so, though, I'll get a med. As always, your <u>comments</u> will be read, even from our favorite e-mailer whose name is Fred, who says he lives in a big ol' shed right near the river where he was bred.

More to come! We'll have more fun! I'm not totally done!

From: **http://www.henryVIII.com/blog/**

Subject: **No Luck with the Ladies**

Luck in love hath never been on the side of King Henry VIII. Even a mere mortal, one without sight into things unseen, is in full knowledge of these things. Alas, those who recall the King's Great Matter and the dissolution of my union with Queen Catherine know quite well that in love, my luck is half that of one who lives with the worst bad luck imaginable.

It has happened again, as I'm sure the loyal readers of your King's script well know by now—but this time 'twas not the fault of yours truly. It seems as though Queen Anne, she who hath no successful pregnancies, has turned out to be a witch, hiding in the shadows. Her powers, it seems, were even too much for a powerful man such as myself, as this normal almost unattractive spellcaster pulled me into her web of deceit, which resulted in a dishonest union between the two of us. You've also heard, I am quite sure, of her adulterous affairs with more than five other individuals and of her desire to injure me when my head was turned. Like I have written prior—once again it seems that the beloved Henry VIII has chosen unwisely.

What are my faults? What is it that drives women away from the space I share with them? What actions do I enact that are so horrible?

I believe I mentioned that I ordered the witch Queen Anne to lose her head in the days to come. No tears will fall from mine eyes, that I can confirm. Of course, 'tis true that her death was commanded by yours truly—and it shall be carried out. It is the least that a monster like Anne deserves!

As for me—I find myself hopeful for another union with a sweet and honourable woman. One who is not afraid to take a chance! I find that my heart is open for yet another!

Did I mention I am an avid dice player? A musician at heart? One who enjoys the art of writing and the crafting of songs that warm the insides of cold, angry men? I am, it seems, looking for another wife to fill the shoes of the two previously whose lives met with dark times . . . yes . . . Indeed. But I would fault thee for letting moments that have once happened affect moments that have yet to occur. A positive future awaits with Henry VIII!

And if such a woman can deliver a newborn son into my life, that would be the most extraordinary result! If she says she can do such things and cannot . . . well, I cannot confirm the outcome of such a situation, but I would attempt to be understanding to the best of my ability.

Women! I await your <u>correspondences</u>!

From: **http://www.wilt_chamberlain.com/counting-up-blog/**

Subject: **14,372, 373, 374, 375, 376, 377, 378 (and maybe 379)**

What up, people!?

Let me just say right now that this week's been crazy busy for me! No! Not the b-ball, but the ladies! Man, how those ladies love the Wilt. This week, I met #14,372 after a b-ball scrimmage, met #14,373 in line for a hot dog, met #14,374 while picking up a dime off the sidewalk, met #14,375 while wiping my windshield clean at the gas station near my pad, met #14,376 while shopping for dental floss at the market, met #14,377 through a mutual friend at a dinner party, and met #14,378 and her sister (which technically should count for 378 AND 379) while callin' a cab.

Maybe you could be #14,380 if you're lucky and get in contact with me by sending a glossy picture that is at least 8 × 10, color, with a list of your hobbies and the kind of music you like to groove to. Married ladies—you're shit outta luck. Like I told ya before, I don't mess with the married ladies. S'like messing with your mother—she's got an old man who'll kick your ass.

I must tell ya, this counting up stuff is gettin' to be a little bit like basketball. You know, you're out there on the court, racking up the points, a free throw here and there. You're watchin' the board and those numbers are goin' up and up and the crowd's goin' crazy over you . . . The higher you go, the more you wanna one-up yourself.

In preparation of continuing the documentation of counting up from 14,379—I have made the Ladies of Wilt Picture Gallery for you to look at. Head on inside and take a look at ladies 1 (aah, the memories) all the way to 14,379! It's like watching history unfold right before your eyes through my eyes!!

In an attempt to continue counting up, I plan on visiting the following locations this week:

• The Free Clinic
• The Bus Stop
• The Alleyway Behind the Arby's
• A Crosswalk

- Under the Stairwell at PS 122
- The Return Line at Sears
- Dental Convention
- Condiment Aisle in Supermarket (in front of the pickles)
- A Random Neighborhood Picked off a Map

If all goes down how I think it will, I'll see you back here next week with new photographs and stories of number 14,380 through 388!

From: **http://www.earlofsandwich.com/ ~johnmontagu/blog**

Subject: **Cleanliness Leads to Godliness**

Grandfather Edward, the 3rd Earl of Sandwich, made it clear to me from the moment whilst I was a small child that cleanliness was key when representing the earldom. With cleanliness comes godliness and respect and honour and position. My habits, which some find repetitive, which may include cleaning beneath my nails and within my hands sometimes ten times a day, have caused me to rise through the ranks and garner respect from others in the House of Lords.

Last night marked the culmination of such respect, when I was appointed as the First Lord of the Admiralty by the King of England! Indeed, a raucous celebration replete with meat and cheese and wine took up most of the evening.

Of course, as the guest of honor, my place was at the head of the table, with no opportunity to leave at any point. Yet, there before me on my place setting, I spied large cuts of beef and cheese ready for the eating! But alas, no cloth in which to wipe my hands, or clean my fingers. I had previously shaken the hands of almost twenty men . . . their hands could have been absolutely anywhere! (I gasp just thinking about such horrors.)

In my attempts to guard my food from the horrific dirt that had since been transferred to the palm of my hand (no thanks to the others), I slid such delicacies upon a slice of bread, giving me an edible platter, if you may, from which to consume the bountiful meal. Yet, of course, balancing such meats atop a flimsy piece of bread was complicated and quickly made me the center of attention. But as the new Lord of the Admiralty, I acted fast, sliding a second piece of bread on top—giving my hands something to grasp upon. Needless to say, the room applauded in excitement as others began to follow my lead in eating this brand-new concoction I had thought up in the heat of the moment!

Many throughout the evening made mention of the new creation, one that stemmed out of an aspiration for cleanliness—and in an attempt to keep such a creation connected to the family name I immediately came up with a rough list of names for the meat and bread meal.

They include: "squishbread," "lotsa meat 'n' cheese," "breadiness," "che-meatatain," "the Monta-googoo," "grabbahand," "John's ultimate creation," "two-sliced goodness oh yeah," "che-meat-again" and my absolute favorite—"The Be-Holden."

I spent a little time taking a poll around the room, but tried not to overshadow the real reason behind everyone's attendance—my new title! In fact, after some time of trying to fully sell "the Monta-googoo," I settled back into the professional persona that the Lord of the Admiralty must exude and I figure that such a creation will end up with a name that I'm sure I won't find silly, annoying or just plain egocentric!

From: **http://www.noah.com/blog**

Subject: **Wanted!**

I'm currently looking to you for help in a very unique matter.

I am in desperate need to find and obtain any or all of the following animals:

- Cow (male and female)
- Platypus (male only)
- Horse (female only)
- Elephant (male and female, gentle temperaments)
- Giraffe (female only)
- Tiger (male and female, babies preferred)
- Octopus (if you can tell me how to figure out if they're male or female, I'd be extremely indebted to you)
- Porcupine (male only)
- Spiders (any and all)
- Hippopotamus (male only)
- Cobra snake (male or female, please deliver in enclosed box for safe transport)
- Dolphin (male or female)
- Owl (male only)
- Kangaroo (male or female)
- Bluebird (male only)
- Frog (female only, nonslimy species)

I am willing to pick up any or all of the above animals no matter the distance. Please contact me if you have any available for this very unique matter in which I am currently involved.

I have been authorized to compensate those who can help me in this matter in a variety of ways which I would be happy to discuss, assuming you do indeed possess any or all of the above of God's wonderful creatures.

Blessings to any and all who read this.

If you have arrived here by way of Lamech's list where I have also listed what I'm looking to obtain, thank you for connecting through. If you would be so kind as to spread the word as quickly as possible, it would be greatly appreciated!

From: **http://www.james_naismith.com/blog/**
Subject: **Wintertime Boredom**

Brrrrr! It's cold!

Springfield, Massachusetts, is, of course, always cold this time of year, but the physical education classes I teach here at the YMCA International Training School are so-called "injured" when the weather turns this time of year. We obviously can't participate in team sports or events outside, and so we're stuck inside. A unique challenge was issued to me, to find something athletic for my students to do inside during this time of the year.

I'm proud to say, I think I've got a wonderful idea!

You remember when I wrote about <u>Duck-on-a-Rock</u>? I used to play it as a kid in Canada . . . You can read more about it <u>here</u> . . . But it got me to thinking that maybe, just maybe, there was a way to create a game for two teams, that involves a ball of some kind, on an indoor court.

With Duck-on-a-Rock, you'd put a baseball in a circle on the ground while others tried to knock that ball out by getting one of their own into the circle. Well, that got me to thinking about just trying to get a ball in a circle, or hoop. And that got me to thinking about putting some kind of hook or basket up really high. To add to the challenge!

And thus, Naismith's Basketball game was born!!

So far, other than having to get the ball in the basket and each team being comprised of nine players, I'm still working on a variety of rules and whatnot. Some of the rules I'm toying with include the following:

1. After making a basket, you must hop on one foot back to your team's side.
2. If you grab on to the basket you are immediately ejected from the game.
3. If you attempt to throw the ball into the basket and someone gets in your way or knocks the ball out of your hand, you get a do-over.
4. One player will be blindfolded on each team, to add to the challenge of the game.

5.   If between the time a ball leaves a player's hands and goes into the basket, all players of the other team yell (in unison) "basket-basket-basketball, if it goes up, then it must fall, hoo-hah, hoo-hah, hoo-hah," then the basket (no matter if it goes in or not) does not count.

These are, of course, just some rules that are in the works. I'm not quite sure about the hopping thing (although it would add to the visual humor of the game), but I'm pretty sure that #5 would be a great way to level the playing field between teams that are extremely athletically talented and those who are just good at chanting rhyming phrases in unison.

As I continue to develop the rules for the game, I'll be posting them here for your input and thoughts.

In the meantime, visit the <u>YMCA's Official Site</u> and my <u>Duck-on-a-Rock Fan Site</u> where you can view pictures of the game as it happens!

More to come.

From: **http://www.franksinatra.com/blog/**

Subject: **This Week's Meme**

<u>Sammy</u>'s gone all crazy this week with the damn meme thing—you know the drill, he throws out some kinda question then all of us here on the <u>Rat Pack Webring</u> gotta answer in our own words. You get me? That's the meme—one question asked to many, who all respond with their own damn answers.

This week, Sammy's all stuck on music (what do you expect with that guy?) and throws out the meme—"Name the 10 songs you're currently groovin' to!" The guy rambles on about other stuff and if you wanna read the post you can check it out on <u>his blog</u>.

As for me—here's my damn answers, Sammy, now leave me the hell alone.

<u>10 Songs I'm Currently Listening To</u>

1. My Way
2. Lady Is a Tramp
3. I've Got You Under My Skin
4. New York, New York
5. Night and Day
6. The Way You Look Tonight
7. Send in the Clowns
8. Love and Marriage
9. Fly Me to the Moon
10. It Was a Very Good Year

Done.

From: **http://www.robert_atkins.com/blog/**

Subject: **The New Diet Revolution**

As I've alluded to in the past, I have been working long and hard on what I believe to be the next revolution in dieting and healthy eating. Doctors around the world all have their beliefs, their food pyramids and quick fixes that one "should incorporate into their lives" to reach the epitome of healthfulness.

The 1960s, of course, have found Americans in a precarious situation with the lines of communication continuing to confuse and misdirect when it comes to a healthful eating plan. What I am about to present to you will revolutionize healthful eating and will, I believe, give Americans (once and for all) the be-all and end-all of successful dieting techniques.

I call it **The Atkins Bread Diet**.

Let's face it. Americans love their carbohydrates. Breads, pastas, cereals, whole grains, potatoes, et cetera. But in eating all these things at once, we cause an excessive secretion of insulin in our systems. This is because we are eating many many different kinds of white flours and carbohydrates. But **The Atkins Bread Diet** removes all those other errant carb-heavy foods and simplifies it for Americans with an easy-to-follow diet that isn't confusing, is pleasant to be on, and results in a slim and healthy figure.

How does it work? I'm sure you're asking yourself.

You eat bread. Any and all kinds of bread. All the time. For breakfast, a few slices of toast, with a sourdough roll on the side. For lunch, garlic bread, bread sticks, sandwiches (without anything in the middle of course). Snacks in the afternoon (to curb your appetite) can include anything from the Atkins special list of bread products—everything from crackers to pizza crusts to sticky buns and French toast. As for dinner—something sensible. Perhaps a croissant or a bagel.

The key is this: **no protein, no sugar, nothing other than bread**.

If you want to eat sixteen loaves of bread for dinner . . . do it! If you want to eat a thousand crackers, have fun! If you want to eat sixteen hundred bagels, have your way with them.

In the end, I believe—if all you eat is bread, you'll be trim and slim and notice a sudden increase in energy.

The Atkins Bread Diet is the revolutionary diet for a new generation and you can order a more detailed pamphlet on the diet by clicking <u>here</u>. A sample eating plan can be viewed <u>here</u>.

Sure, I have ideas for other diets—but I think this one has the true potential to really change the way we think about eating! I'm sure it will do the same for you, too!

From: **http://www.blogs.fr/~marie_antoinette/**

Subject: **Royal Appearances #43**

I am quite certain that the recent sightings of the royals far exceeds the previous week's events! It is, to say the least, quite enlightening!

It's no surprise that **Louis XVI** was spotted being fitted for a brand-new crown this week in Paris and I was there to witness it all. Although the previous one, bejeweled and affixed with some of the most costly accoutrements ever, it has been rumored that XVI was heard to say, "Is this all?" Apparently, some Kings prefer their heads to be weighted down with the fortunes of a thousand kingdoms so that fatigue far outweighs their desire for physical intimacy with their Queens!

Fashion designer **Rose Bertin** was seen visiting the exclusive château, La Petit Trianon, mere days ago—rumors have it that she's designing an elegant gown for none other than, well . . . **Queen Marie Antoinette**. Although details have yet to be revealed as for what event such a stunning gown should be created, murmurs point to a special Parisian opera ball, mere days away.

Rumors are swirling around royal palaces here in France that **Louis XVI** may very well consider appointing the **duc de Guines** as France's ambassador to England. While it is no surprise that Guines happens to be close acquaintances with none other than **me**, it is apparent that yours truly has no influence in this matter. For Guines, who would make a magnificent ambassador, we here at <u>Marie Antoinette's Royal Appearances</u> suspect that the deed may be done before you've finished reading these writings!

Short takes: **Madame Campan**, this week, joins the Queen's staff as one of her ladies-in-waiting. **Artois** visits the Paris Opera in disguise! **Thérèse de Lamballe** is being considered for the Superintendent of the Queen's Household! Gambling at Versailles was a certain **Queen** who was said to have walked away with a huge fortune (but we won't say just who it was for fear of angering the peasants)! **Emperor Joseph II** is seen in a serious discussion with none other than **Louis XVI**—what's that all about!?

As always, the daily gossip and scandals will appear as they happen here on <u>Marie Antoinette's Royal Appearances Weblog</u> for your entertainment and informational purposes only.

As gossip is never completely reliable, please do not hold me responsible for anything you read here, as the details may not be fully legitimate.

Spotted a royal doing something strange? Something illegal? Something lascivious? Send your tips to tips@royalappearances.fr! Anonymity will be preserved!

From: **http://www.pavlov.com/**

From: **http://www.ian_fleming.com/blog/**

Subject: **New Jobs, New Opportunities**

Indeed, I've received quite a handful of ribbings as of late, for my lack of prolific writing here on this digital space. Rightfully so, such ribbings could never take into consideration my current status as a stockbroker at Rowe and Pitman here in Bishopsgate. A status of which I am none too pleased.

Of course, the reason for my writing today is to inform my readers that a change is on its way. Yes, you have probably noticed that I took my CV down off this site (that link is now inoperable) due to the fact that I have been offered a position working as the personal assistant to John Godfrey—the Director of Naval Intelligence of the Royal Navy.

What does such a position mean for yours truly?

Above all, it means that finally my studies at the Sandhurst military academy will come into play, and that I will have to relocate for the position. The animals of the house will be less than pleased with the change of scenery.

My miniature poodle, "Dr. No"—whom I named after my physician who refused to prescribe medication for my headaches (and which I previously wrote about here)—is still as stubborn as always, and will most likely refuse to even leave this place behind. As for "Moneypenny," my cockatiel (whom you remember I won in a night of gambling from an individual who was short, by one single pound) should have no problem, as her cage is all that matters to her. My rat with the single miscolored digit, "Goldfinger," well . . . as long as there's cheese he's up for the lot of it all.

But alas, the calico kitten that goes by the name of "Bonda" (after the South Indian snack made of deep-fried potatoes) will be the easiest of them all, as he is always able to fit in, in any foreign situations. I must say, I sometimes wish I had the ability to blend like little Bonda does. He is just the smoothest of all the Fleming family members.

I do have a good feeling about the relocation and the new position, however—it will give me a great opportunity in which to learn more about the politics behind such a governmental organization . . . It fascinates me . . . mostly because I'm quite sure there are stories worth telling whose inspiration lies in a real-world environment such as that.

As always, you can keep in touch with me by sending correspondence here. I will not abandon you, that is for sure—but it may be some time before I can write again.

From: **http://www.13colonies.com/~samuel_adams/**

Subject: **Failing Old Samuel**

Those who follow these trivial matters may recall the dark times that befell the Adams family in 1748—upon which my father and the patriarch of the Adams family, Old Samuel Adams, allowed death to do him in. Family responsibility stepped in, and yours truly took over the reins of the family brewery.

I fear as though all my hard work has now been for naught—as our brewery, that which I have attempted to draw success to, looks to be on its final legs. And so, here I sit, preparing to shut down that which brought Old Samuel such joy, sixteen years after his passing.

What follows such a low moment? I have wondered. Some suggest that an education from Harvard College should leave me in the best of situations. That while a brewery might have been a possible pathway in life, that a new direction is not wholly strange or inappropriate. It is thoughts and suggestions like these that direct me toward politics, where I believe a difference can fully be made—especially when such a difference can be made in response to the harmful legislature being levied by the supreme magistrate.

Then again, my instincts go back to that of the brewery. Many suggest that our family was never meant to run a successful brewery . . . That lager and ale had no place alongside the Adams name . . . That politics and government and education were our destiny.

Still, I cannot help but wonder if years down the line I will find myself regretting the abandonment of such a business opportunity. That someone else will take such an idea and use it to great effect, while I find myself mired in legal papers and problematic issues . . .

Maybe tea. Maybe there's something for Samuel Adams in the business of tea.

Perhaps.

In the meantime, the brewery has two months left before the doors are shut—if you so feel determined to savor our product, you must act quickly. For after this, your chance of sampling a lager under the name Samuel Adams will never come again!

Of that, I am sure.

From: **http://www.abbottandcostello.com/blog/**
Subject: **Our Newest Blog Comedy Routine**

Hey folks, Abbott here! Wanted to thank all our great fans for supporting us over the years by giving you the first look at our new comedy sketch! We think you'll like it. But if you don't, don't send me any thoughts to abbott@acprods.com.

Abbott: *So, technology is pretty amazin', isn't it, Costello?*
Costello: *You know it, boss.*
Abbott: *The way people can share their thoughts from their own personal diaries . . .*
Costello: *I don't wanna read any of your personal thoughts. That scares me.*
Abbott: *Oh, relax! The thing is, you gotta get a whole buncha things goin' before you can just start writin'.*
Costello: *Oh yeah? I didn't know that. Like what?*
Abbott: *Well, you need an I.P. address.*
Costello: *I don't know about you, but I know where I pee and I don't need any stinkin' address to fig'r that out!*
Abbott: *No, Costello—not your home address . . . You gotta let people know that URL!*
Costello: *First of all, I'm not the one askin' you to tell people where you pee—and second of all, I'm not the one who's ill! You are ill! Not me!*
Abbott: *Costello . . .*
Costello: *What.*
Abbott: *I didn't say you were sick. URL!*
Costello: *What, like mentally ill?*
Abbott: *No, Costello, not mentally ill.*
Costello: *You're telling me that in order to share my own thoughts with the public . . .*
Abbott: *Go on . . .*
Costello: *I gotta . . . give out my "I pee address" and give 'em the ol' . . .*
Abbott: *URL thing.*
Costello: *And I'm sacrificin' my own career and doing this for what reason?*
Abbott: *To get comments.*
Costello: *To get comments?*
Abbott: *Yes. If you let people know your I.P. address and that URL . . . People will come and leave comments.*
Costello: *And tell me that I'm a deranged lunatic, most likely for telling them that I pee.*

Abbott: *Whether or not you tell 'em you're a deranged lunatic is your own business, Costello . . . I'm not gonna tell you how to live your life!*

Costello: *But you are!*

Abbott: *I'm just telling you how to get people to read what you have to say. To get you a whole bunch of hits.*

Costello: (Flinches here) *Who's gonna hit me?*

Abbott: *Not hit you . . . Hits.*

Costello: *So, more than one person is gonna hit me?*

Abbott: *Well, if you're lucky—hundreds and thousands.*

Costello: *What!?!?*

Abbott: *It's a good thing, Costello.*

Costello: *I don't know what kind of world you're livin' in, buddy boy, but I don't consider having people come to my I pee address and watch me and tell me I'm ill and leave me comments and hit me . . . to be a good thing.*

Abbott: *Well, it's better than spam.*

Costello: *I like Spam.*

Abbott: *You don't have spam.*

Costello: *Well, I've had Spam.*

Abbott: *Once you have spam, you always have spam.*

Costello: *I had Spam last Christmas, then didn't have Spam until Easter.*

Abbott: *You had spam in December, then no spam until April!? That's not possible.*

Costello: *Ask my mother!*

Abbott: *What does your mother know about spam!?*

Costello: *That's her business! She makes sure everyone in my family gets Spam!*

Abbott: *Well, Costello—I can't say I was ever more disappointed in your mother than at this very moment.*

Costello: *That's not very nice.*

Abbott: (Deep sigh here) *Here's the thing, Costello. If you don't want hits . . .*

Costello: *No, I don't want hits!*

Abbott: *And you won't give out your I.P. address or let people know that URL . . .*

Costello: *I refuse! I ain't no sicko!*

Abbott: *Then the only other way is to give out links to others . . .*

Costello: *First Spam, now sausage links! You hungry or something?*

Abbott: *I'm not talking food, Costello. I'm talking links.*

Costello: *Well, I don't know what country you live in my friend, but where I come from—links ARE food.*

Abbott: *I guess, figuratively, that's sorta true.*

Costello: *You betcha bipper!*

Abbott: *Well then, Costello —I'm not gonna tell you how or where to give out those links. You do what you wanna do.*

Costello: *I will! And I ain't givin' nobody nothing, just to come and read what I gotta say. They can come if they want, or they don't hafta. But I ain't getting hit, givin' out food, or tellin' them that I'm sick or even telling them that you are ill!*

Abbott: *Well, I'm sure they don't care if you're sick or not . . . But they do wanna know that URL.*

Costello: *Which I'm not!*

Abbott: *Not, what?*

Costello: *Ill!*

Abbott: *I never said you were ill.*

Costello: *You did, just then!*

Abbott: *You're scaring me, Costello.*

Costello: *Aggggghhhh!!! I think I'm havin' a heart attack!*

Abbott: *So, then you ARE ill!*

(Costello faints. Abbott picks him up and drags him offstage.)

From: **http://www.salvador_dali.com/blog/**

From: **http://www.patton.com/~george/blog/**

Subject: **Give Up? Never!**

Pardon my French, but this is all a bunch of bullshit!

Hell, I don't care what you think about my words as long as it gets through your sickening, thick skulls! There's a war out there raging . . . A war that's taking its toll . . . Communication is breaking down, and without communication—a cohesive group of men can't fight their way outta a piss-soaked paper bag.

I'm talkin' about all these crybaby wimps who joined the Army's <u>Blogging Webring</u> where all they had to do over the course of a year was throw something up once a week for their troops . . . A quick update, a quick note. Somethin' to keep morale high—because without morale we might as well all go home and stick our heads in the friggin sand and wait for someone to blow our asses through our mouths.

Left and right, I've seen it. All these crybabies, givin' up on the blogging. Long posts and passages dedicated to "not having the time to blog," "not feeling creative enough to blog," "not having hands, which were shot off in battle, and not being able to blog" . . .

It's a bunch of goddamn bullshit if you ask me.

You don't give up because you aren't feeling it. In war, you don't wake up one day and tell your commanding officer that you're not gonna fight because, well, you just don't have the time or because you didn't expect it to be this much work. No! So, if you don't do that on the battlefield, after committing to this Army project, how can you do the same thing? In fact, all over, and it ain't just enlisted men—these pansies are givin' up at every turn because they just aren't feeling it.

I say to these fools, you might as well shoot yourself in the head while you're at it—because if you give up this damn quickly when the going gets tough . . . Well, then, I don't want you backing me up out there in the real battle.

Not feelin' creative? No time to do it? Want to give up on your blog? Well, go ahead! But don't write me some boring, tired, long article about why. Because if you're giving up, everything you're writing about is bullshit anyway. Give up and go away or stick with it and be a man!!

Stand up to the fear and the second-guessing and the lack of confidence! Stand up to your ability to be overcome by laziness. Stand up and do something and get that thing written.

Maybe then, someone will give you some goddamn respect!

From: **http://www.edgarallanpoe.com/blog/**

Subject: **The Visitor, Part 23**

I've attempted to contact the local animal control authorities three times on this day, without any luck whatsoever.

If you've stuck with my ramblings over the last two weeks, you have most likely been privy to that which has caused a great deal of stress in my household. My initial description of the events in question can be found here and here. Simply put, the most troublesome of all flapping creatures found its way into my home through an opening in the outer structure—and has been the cause of quite a bit of chaos over the last ten days.

At first, the rapping and tapping echoed throughout my chamber—the kind of knocking which resembled a human hand. I peered through the door many times those first few days, constantly at odds with my work and my obsession in finding out which pint-size rascals of the neighborhood were trying to pull the so-called wool over my eyes.

But before long it became clear to me that a flapping creature had found its way into my attic through a hole in the chimney. And as irony usually presents itself, the hole was too small for me, yet just small enough for our little ebony friend. There has been knocking and tapping and rapping and scratching and screeching and scraping and it is about to drive me to madness.

My writing, it seems, does not benefit from the repetitive sounds being offered forth by this creature whom I cannot dis-patch. My writing, it appears, cannot find its voice as long as another living creature resides above my head. The madness it instills . . . The tapping in my skull . . .

I must attempt at contacting those who can help me, once again, in this matter. Do you know of a solution to get rid of the clapping and rapping and tapping that plagues me ever more? Send a note <u>here</u> if you have a solution that may be quite sure. I must dispatch my ebony friend or else the distraction will most definitely cause my work to suffer.

For what literary masterpiece can come from such pedestrian problems?

From: **http://www.mozart.de/blog/**

Subject: **European Tour Continues . . .**

I've not found the time to write as of late, and for that I apologize—but it has been almost a year away from home while on tour in Europe. This tour has monopolized my time and caused me to neglect that which you are reading now.

I will be performing in London in a matter of days, but I have spent the last few hours updating the <u>concert music files</u> for your listening pleasure. There are some wonderful shows available to listen to, including my performances in <u>Munich</u> and <u>Mannheim</u>.

The <u>Mozart Message Board</u> has been filled with questions regarding my future plans, which I have not had the time to answer until today. If curiosity has gotten the better of you, click <u>here</u> for an audiocast that you may listen to at your own convenience. I will attempt to record and provide audiocasts on a monthly basis through the remaining months of my European tour, so that you may all keep up to date on what's happening with me and my music.

You may or may not have read <u>Salieri's Blog</u>, which contains unauthorized links to audio files of my performances. I personally have not visited the site, but I have heard it is poorly designed, has a lack of interesting features, and there is jealousy running rampant through his words. I'll advise all of those who are looking to listen to the music of Mozart to visit my <u>music vault</u> and listen to the performances in the quality they were meant to be heard. Rogue copies of my music, as presented by Salieri, do not do justice to the music—instead, giving you a lesser product whose tone (I'm quite sure) does not live up to these crystal-clear versions of my performances.

The act of providing what amounts to unauthorized copies of an artist's music seems to be a criminal act of sorts—and those who freely acquire the files of my music in such a way should be held responsible for such actions as well. If you want to experience the music of Mozart, purchase a ticket and come to see a performance instead of taking part in Salieri's less than respectful offerings. (That is all I will say on the subject of acquiring illegal music files.)

Finally, I must put to rest the rumors that seem to flow freely from a variety of European gossip sites that I am a crude, promiscuous, unrefined dolt. I do not deny my love for women, of course! How I would be lying to suggest such things. But crude? Promiscuous? Unrefined?

Well, maybe there is some truth to it all!

Hope to see all of you at my next performance in London!

From: **http://www.johnwayne_gacy.com/blog/**
Subject: **Happy Haikus for a Clown!**

Circus dogs. Balloons.
Jokes and pratfalls and laughter.
Tee hee hee. Tee hee.

Da-da, da-da-dum!
Can you hear the circus song?
I'm dancing! I am!

Working 9 to 5.
A way to make a living.
Having a job sucks.

I'm a happy clown.
I'm happy on the outside.
But on the inside?

Red paint and white paint.
Yay! I like to paint my face!
Hey! Stay in the lines!

Just 'cause I'm a clown,
Doesn't mean I need a dog.
It's a one-man show!

Where is the laughter?
Why have they forsaken me?
Poor pitiful clown.

The balloons have popped.
I let all of the air out.
Don't try to stop me.

Cotton candy! Yum!
Do you like cotton candy?
You'd better like it.

Any thoughts on JWG's haikus? Send me your contact information, along with your address, phone number, daily schedule, social security number, and I'll come to you.

From: **http://www.martinlutherkingjr.com/dreamblog/**

Subject: **Today's Dream.**

I had a dream . . .

A dream that, well, now that I find myself trying to share this dream here on
martinlutherkingjr.com, I find my memory does not serve me in the way I wish it would.

I had a dream . . .

. . . filled with visions so much like paradise, that while I slept I believed that such images were
real and concrete . . . Images I awoke from, images that I rose up from having, images that besides
the general "paradise" theme, I have no idea what they were.

I had a dream . . .

I'm sure it had nothing to do with falling, like this dream, and I'm fairly certain it had nothing to
do with my children, like that dream. Sometimes if I just sit here and try to empty my thoughts I
can come up with the subject matter of the dream at hand so all my friends and family and readers can tell me what they believe the significance could be . . . But today, as I write these words,
dear friends, all I can tell you is that—

I had a dream . . . One which my mind can't grasp or remember. I had this dream last night, and
yet today it is a mere shadow of a fully realized world of the night before. Sure, every once in a
while when I'm doing something like brushing my teeth or buttering a piece of bread I get a flash
of the dream, and then it's gone like it had never been there in the first place!

I had a dream and recall awakening in the dark of the night, sitting up with my dream log and
turning on the light and attempting to find my way to the pen on my bedside table so that I could
write down the images and the elements so that when the daylight came, I would be able to write
those images here for all to see. So that we could, together, share that vision and dissect it . . .

What symbolism did such a dream contain? Did it contain images of water, wind, walls or guns?
Did it communicate through me my stresses and concerns and worries? Would the lessons of
such a dream help me in my waking life, in combating those who seek to stand strong against the
civil rights movement as it pertains to the freedom of all who stand in my corner?

I had a dream . . . but that doesn't mean I'm ever going to remember it.

In the meantime, maybe you'd enjoy checking out my <u>previous dreams</u>, which include the <u>one in which I am falling off a tall building in Alabama and then land in the ocean where I swim around with the fish</u> or the <u>dream where I'm playing a tuba and flute at the same time while hopping on one foot and singing "She'll Be Comin' 'Round the Mountain"</u> or the <u>dream where I eat a thousand hamburgers</u>.

Peace.

From: **http://www.florence_nightingale.com/blog/**

Subject: **Party to a Wounded Dog**

Mother and Father had the most exquisite social engagement of the season yesterday evening, with most of the well-to-do around London arriving in ornate carriages and bearing wonderful gifts for the family. Mother told me I would have to stay upstairs during the event, as it was for the elder members and not for children like me and sister.

We watched from the window upstairs as people came and went that afternoon, trying hard to keep our eyes open as the night enveloped the sky—of course, we were startled when deep into the evening we heard the sound of a crying dog in the distance. We rushed down in our nightgowns onto the front drive—and there we spotted a dog that a carriage had hit.

I took one look at the blood and blacked out.

Mother was standing over me, holding my cold palm when my eyes opened again—but all I could see was the poor dog's wounds and it made me so sick that I couldn't bear to keep my eyes open. I cried and I cried (although my sister did not) and my mother and father assured me that the dog had not suffered and was now in a better place.

But the blood. I could not keep myself from thinking about it. Seeing it. The oozing red thickness of it all permeated my thoughts. It was a living nightmare for me, and although Mother and Father have done their best to wipe the image from my mind, I must be candid when I say that if I never see such things ever again in my lifetime, it will not be too soon.

Social engagements and Sunday tea. These are the things that I find myself longing for. The simplicity of life without complication. The pure paradise of living a life where you are safe, taken care of and satisfied. This is what Mother and Father will provide for me and sister—and these are the images that I hold close as the events of yesterday still cloud my mind.

I shiver with horror. Blood. There can be nothing less appealing than that!

Sister, of course, has already begun <u>talking about yesterday's events</u> on her own journal, where she revels in the events by providing sketches of the incident. I, personally, have not gazed upon them nor will I choose to do so . . . I must put such horrific images as far from my mind as possible!

From: http://www.mao_zedong.ch/blog/

Subject: You Will Read This Blog, Repeatedly (As Written by Chairman Mao)

You have come here to my weblog because it has been required of you.

 First, if you have not <u>purchased the "Little Red Book"</u> filled with helpful quotations from a variety of my speeches, you must do so now.

Click on the image of my book to the left and order it now. It is required that each citizen own my book and thus there should be no delay in your clicking of the image to the left here on my official site and purchasing the book so you may carry it with you wherever you go and that which you will show to others who do not yet have it so you may influence them to purchase my book as well. Once again, this is required of all citizens by law, and thus, you must buy it.

Wonderful news!! My book, *Quotations from Chairman Mao Zedong* is currently the #1 bestseller in China! Some are saying that the book, which some refer to as the "Little Red Book," has surpassed the Bible in sales and that it appears as if each and every citizen has one in their home. This is wonderful news, and a total surprise, and I can't thank enough each and every citizen who has decided, on their own, to pick up this book!

Now that we have finished with the above business, which I remind you is your duty to purchase, I would like to direct your attention to a variety of additional writings not included in the above book (but which will be included in *More Quotations from Chairman Mao Zedong*, and a potential follow-up book entitled *Even More Quotations from Chairman Mao Zedong*) . . . You will want to click on these articles because I am asking you to and if at some point in the near future you are questioned on the words within these writings and you cannot answer such questions, well, these will be dark times for both you . . . and you.

<u>Why I Like Swimming, Pt 1</u>
<u>Why I Like Swimming, Pt 2</u>
<u>Building a Pool Near the Forbidden City, Pt 1</u>
<u>A Pool Is Born!</u>
<u>Class Struggle, and Swimming</u>
<u>Why We'd Rather Not Fight a War, and Swim Instead</u>

It would be wise for all who read this page (which should include every citizen of our country) to send a message <u>here</u> and include text that praises the words that I have provided above, as well as the book that some are saying "is sweeping the nation of China"!

A #1 bestseller! I am beside myself with glee.

From: **http://www.evabraun.com/blog/**

Subject: **An Exciting Time!**

You will not believe what happened to me this week . . .

So I'm working for Heinrich Hoffmann—he's that photographer I told you about <u>here</u> who takes photographs of the Nazi Party . . . Well, I went out to assist him the other night and something amazing happened . . .

I met the most wonderful, gentlemanly, intriguing man ever—such a mysterious fellow who goes by the nickname "Herr Wolff"! He comes across as a total gentleman, although some may say he looks a bit silly with his funny mustache and his big felt hat! But that's what's so refreshing compared to the evil men I've dated before—this "Wolff" is different! He's not a man in wolf's clothing, but a "Wolff" of a man! Like you've all said before—it's time for Eva to find a nice gentleman this time around anyway! <u>Franz112@gestal.de</u> said it best when he wrote that *"Eva should find a man who cares about others, who wears his heart on his sleeve and who can laugh at himself!"*

Well, Franz—I believe I've fallen for a man just like that!

Sure, my father and family disagree with Adolf's (that's his real name, isn't it so adorable!?) political beliefs and whatnot—but really, when have someone's political beliefs ever harmed anyone? When love is in the air, isn't that the most important thing between a man and a woman? Isn't that all that one should take into consideration?

<u>Beatrice@gestal.de</u> wrote me a note that said, *"Eva—when you find that gentle, supportive, loving gentleman that you are looking for to complete your life, you will know it! Do not listen to anyone else around you—they don't have your best interests at heart! If you feel it. If it makes you feel happy . . . Then it is what you should pursue!"*

I did something silly, too. After meeting him and finding myself enamored with him and his silly little outfit, I slipped him a love letter into his pocket! I know!!! So crazy! But I felt that we were meant for each other from that simple meeting and could not let him disappear forever without at least letting him know my true feelings!

I can just tell—this is going to so work out and my family will get to really know him and realize how great of a person I feel that he is . . . They'll finally realize that my instinct in picking someone (this time) is good. That I've gotten better at really seeking out the kind, thoughtful, harmless partner that will share a long life with me, forever!

God, I'm so giddy about the future right now I can't even stand it!

From: **http://www.ferdinand_marcos.ph/blog/**

Subject: **Problems Other than Martial Law**

I understand some are not pleased that on September 21 I declared martial law here in the Philippines, as supported by Proclamation No. 1081. But understand that such decision was motivated by the current violent activities by the New People's Army (their website is here). I promise to try and make this drastic change in governmental policy as seamless as possible.

Under these new guidelines, I will be introducing my vision of "Bagong Lipunan" or, a new society—a new direction in which all people (no matter their class, background or wealth) will work together toward the common goal of achieving the liberation of the Filipino people. The first step, of course, will involve a redistribution of wealth, so to speak . . . Families with great wealth will have their property given to those with less. Those with privately held land will find that some will be given elsewhere. It is important that those who stockpile their wealth or spend inordinate amounts of money on useless items and/or worthless material goods should not flaunt such financial status and waste such wealth while others are starving or necessitating more.

This is, of course, the focus of Bagong Lipunan.

In other news, I must direct you to Imelda's Shoe Fantasy—a new site she's just created which includes over 3,000 pictures of her extremely large collection of shoes and lingerie. You'll especially want to peruse her unique pieces in the collection—from her pair of plastic disco sandals whose heels flash while one dances (which cost $2,500) to her bulletproof bra (valued at over $10,000)!! Imelda is quite adept at providing commentary on each pair of shoes and each brassiere—from where she bought them to how much they cost, to how many times she has worn them (usually fewer than two times, can you believe it!?) and why each pair means so much to her. It's a wonderful site with a great message—that fashion really can make you happy!

Once again, we will get through this period of civil and violent unrest—this martial law will play its part, fix the problem, and return the Philippines to a place where all citizens will be able to afford a comfortable lifestyle and where those who take advantage of their wealth will be treated to a reality they will soon not forget!

Bagong Lipunan!

From: **http://www.spiritofsaintlouis.com/lindbergh/**

Subject: **Blogging the Transatlantic Flight**

Pre-flight, Roosevelt Airfield, NYC: Press. Family. Friends. Levity and excitement all around. This is going to be such a wonderful opportunity—being the very first person to fly solo from New York to Paris. I'm a little nervous, but we've double-checked everything. Departure is minutes away. Shared a quiet moment with the plane's designer, <u>Donald Hall</u>.

Hour 1 & 2: The great going-away celebration at Roosevelt Field still has me smiling. Wow. Just an amazing opportunity. Reflecting some more on the departure. On the flawless takeoff. Should probably go over my flight plan and check over the instrument panel.

Hour 3: Checking over the instrument panel some more. Everything looks okay. Spending more time thinking about departure in NYC. That was a great moment. All those people. It's a little quiet being alone up here. No one to talk to. I had some great conversations while in NYC on the airstrip. Talked to some of the technicians from Ryan Airlines—the company that built the plane. That was fun.

Hour 4: Sooooooooooooooo, yeah. Umm . . . Did I mention that when we took off from Roosevelt Field it was a pretty flawless takeoff? Yeah. That was great. Yeah.

Hour 5: It's been the fifth hour for what seems like ten hours. I have about twenty-eight more hours to go until we reach, er, until "I" reach Paris. I should have brought a book. Although, if I think back to when I took off from Roosevelt Field, maybe I can replay it in my mind like I'm watching a movie. Maybe that would keep me busy or entertain me and make the time fly? Maybe not. That's just stupid. Concentrating on the flight. That's the most important thing.

Hour 6: And then Donald Hall says, "*It's been such a pleasure working with you, Charles.*" And then I say, "*Thanks, Donald.*" And then he says, "*I wish you the best of luck, and my thoughts are with you.*" And then I say, "*Yes, but what about the Russians!?*" And he looks at me with this look of horror and says, "*The Russians? Have they found us out!?*" And then there's this big explosion and we go running for cover.

Hour 12: I thought I saw a Model T up here with me after Donald Hall and I battled and successfully escaped from the Russians who were intent on stealing my plane for questionable and treasonous activities. I tried to follow the Model T, which brought me off course, which I've now rectified. Twenty-one more hours to go.

Hour 15: I can see the Eiffel Tower. I swear to God I can see the Eiffel Tower. Yes, I know it's far away and yes, I know it shouldn't be possible, but I am telling you I can see the Eiffel Tower. I mean, sure I have great eyesight—I'm always able to see that line on the very bottom of the eye chart . . . it's E, E, E, E, a backwards E, and a few more Es. No, there's the Eiffel Tower! I must be closer than I thought. I must be. I swear. I'll be right back.

Hour 17: Back! I'm feeling refreshed and fully in control. There was a moment there where I think I was getting a little bit stir-crazy from being alone for so long on my own in this can. I've checked my progress, and I am glad to say that the *Spirit of St. Louis* is now just over halfway through this amazing journey. Donald took over flying for a while and he's still flying right now. He's an amazing pilot and a truly great friend. Oh wait, he's saying something.

Hour 20: Charles has asked me to impart my design wisdom to those reading these entries. I am both honored and extremely pleased to be assisting Mr. Lindbergh in such a way. Charles and I go way back if you must know, our histories intertwining like a wall of ivy gripping the sides of a tall, brick two-story home. I would fancy a cup of tea at the moment but I'm afraid such a thing isn't possible.

Hour 21: No more . . . No more writing . . .

Hour 22: Hahahahahahahaha.

Hour 23: ad;ljkdafp82-fadkh;d. a;dfkjlds;LHJD ; ;ADSLKF9283(*Y&(*)7B AD;LKJHDLFKHAD.

From: **http://www.edward_r_murrow.com/blog/**

McCARTHY'S COMMUNIST WITCH HUNT
MURROW REPORT

HYDROGEN BOMB TESTED . . . LOCALS REACT!

WHERE IS BIKINI ATOLL ISLAND? DEVELOPING . . .

NNN RADIO STATUS REPORT

"QUEEN ELIZABETH WAS HERE!" SAY AUSTRALIAN LAW-MAKERS DURING LATEST VISIT . . .

HEAR IT NOW SEE IT NOW

HERB MUSCHEL'S P.R. NEWSWIRE . . .

UK GOLD MARKET OPENS . . .

PROBLEMS WITH AMERICAN MOTORS?

BERLIN CONFERENCE FALLOUT!

POLIO VACCINATION SHORTAGES . . . DEVELOPING . . .

REPORT ON SENATOR JOSEPH MCCARTHY TRANSCRIPTS HERE . . .

KNOCK OUT! JOEY G. SLAMS WILLIE TORY . . .

CANADA OPENS FIRST SUBWAY!

60 DAYS WITH DIMAGGIO AND MONROE . . .

MONROE CRIES!

MCCARTHY LIES TO U.S. PUBLIC

AN END TO THE RED SCARE

Send News Tips to Murrow (Anonymity Guaranteed)
SUBMIT HERE

From: **http://www.charliechaplin.com/blog/**

Subject: **Modern Films, Modern Times**

There is a certain beauty to silence.

Peaceful. Quiet. Reflective. Two people, enveloped in such, will often find that their unspoken expressions speak louder than any words they could possibly muster. Silence, in my opinion, is the loudest joy I have ever not heard.

Modern Times arrives in movie houses this week—and it is the first film in which I utter a spoken phrase. Mind you, this is a silent film. There are, yes, mechanized sounds that pipe through speakers during the film, but the actors (myself, <u>Paulette Goddard</u>, <u>Henry Bergman</u>, <u>Stanley Sandford</u> and <u>Chester Conklin</u>) never say a word. At the very end of the film, which you will have to sit through to see, I utter gibberish that can be heard on the limited audio track—but contrary to popular belief this is not symbolic of Charlie Chaplin starting to make "talkies."

The talkies are nothing but a passing fad. I'm well aware of the awards and honors being given to films that have jumped on the wagon of sound . . . But for "The Tramp" this is not the world for him. He communicates through actions. Through expressions. Through body movement. When "The Tramp" embraces sound, and begins to talk, well—there is nothing left of the Tramp that the public has loved. If the Tramp were to speak, he would have no reason to move. And without movement, there is no comedy.

So, yes—I will continue to make silent films as long as I can, and I believe that if I can continue to make films that I am proud of, that so too will the public embrace such movies and abandon these loud, technological monsters that are the current flavor of the month.

If you would like to be kept updated as to my next film, as well as finding information about *Modern Times*, please join the <u>Official Chaplin online club</u> and you'll get a special gift sent to you at home (a replica shoe from *The Gold Rush* that is actually edible!).

And go see *Modern Times* so I can continue making films starring your favorite character, "The Tramp" (<u>Official Tramp Page</u>).

From: **http://www.joanofarc-site.org/blog/**

Subject: **Holy Words**

In God's name, this holy place has been constructed—where God's words can flow through me. This is His plan and I am but merely a vessel for His blessed goals.

On His behalf, Saint Michael the Archangel appeared to me in a vision, telling me that I should communicate these holy words with the people of France in such a place which was denoted as www.joanofarc.fr. It seems, unfortunately, that Saint Michael had been unaware that one had already secured such a name. Saint Catherine and Saint Margaret came to me in a vision soon thereafter, suggesting that since www.joanofarc.fr was already taken, that www.joanofarc-site.fr would be more than acceptable to the Lord. Unfortunately, as God is my witness, one had already acquired www.joanofarc-site.fr and so I once again contacted Saint Michael the Archangel, who suggested www.thejoanofarcultimatesite.fr, which was also taken. In the end, the Lord provides— and as you are here you have seen that www.joanofarc-site.org was available to me.

And so, in God's name, I acted. Seek, and ye shall find. Read, and thou shall understand. Act, and God will act. I act with His words as my defense.

God has commanded me to drive the English out of France. This is my mission and I must communicate as such to the Dauphin. This is, as it seems, a complicated request for a woman such as myself with only sixteen years behind her . . . Even more complicated, as I must find an escort who will take me to his court at Chinon. This is something that seems, at first, to be an unreasonable thing to ask of me. But if I am sent by God, the King of Heaven . . . to ensure that such events are carried out—there is no denying the Almighty.

If you are a soldier or an individual who shares my dedication to the Lord and who would accept the mission of accompanying me through Burgundian-controlled territory to the Dauphin's court in Chinon—please contact me through a vision, or if e-mail is easier: joan@joanofarc-site.org.

I am not afraid, nor should you be. The lot of us have been chosen by God to drive the English out of France. By joining me on this journey you will be fulfilling the plans of the Almighty—who hath predicted the events which I shall be involved with.

From: **http://rockhudson.bloggers.com/**

Subject: **Pillow Talk**

Pillow Talk is now in theaters everywhere!!

It's my first picture with Doris Day, and if I can be so bold—she is one extremely sexy lady! I mean, you can't look at that golden blond hair and that perfect smile and those long, long legs (watch out, fellas!) and tell me that she isn't one of the most beautiful actresses you've ever seen! God knows, I forgot some of my lines because I just couldn't stop looking at this adorable woman!

If you don't know, *Pillow Talk* is a really great romantic comedy which tells the story of a man (me) and a woman (Doris) who find that they hate each other after having to share a telephone line—but as you can imagine, we eventually fall in love! (Thank God, I'd hate to do a movie where I didn't end up getting the girl!)

Did you know that Doris started out as a dancer? Well, of course you did! I mean, dancers have a certain body type (ladies, stop reading and join me and the boys at the end of this page) that, well, is fit for activity! And Doris, she is oh so hot! A few days on the set I thought I was getting sick because I felt like I had a fever but you know what!? That wasn't any fever, boys—that was Doris making me feel that way. All weak-kneed and everything! All I can say is just . . . WOWWOWWOW!

Now don't get me wrong—a lot of you are going to say, "But what about Elizabeth Taylor, Rock?" Well, you know that Elizabeth is just one of the most beautiful women on the face of the earth (and maybe I had a little experience with her, wink wink), but I just have to say that I am completely in love with Doris Day—she just makes me feel like I've never felt before! Now, don't get your gossip mills all up in a twist—we're not IN LOVE in real life, but I'm just saying that a girl as beautiful and sexy as Doris was just a huge pleasure to work with and, well, you go see the movie and you'll agree with me, men. She is, in a word, amazing!!

Before I head out to play some golf and visit a few of my lady friends (don't tell Doris!), I wanna give a shout out to a few blogs of some of my good, close friends: There's <u>Billy</u>, <u>Frank</u>, <u>Emilio</u>, <u>Juan</u>, <u>George</u>, <u>James</u>, <u>Carl</u> and our close buddy we call <u>The Sombrero</u>. Ha! Don't ask! Just visit their sites and tell 'em that the ol' Rock said hello!

From: **http://www.manfredvonrichthofen.de/redbaronblog/**

Subject: **Ratta-tat Ratta-tat Ratta-tat**

Der röte Kampfflieger strikes again! Oh, I am sorry to my poor sad readers who do not speak the superior German language. Let me rephrase for you!

Hello, you Frenchmen! With your pitiful little flying planes that cannot outrun me or escape my bullets! To you, le Diable Rouge is here to shoot you down! Oh, you are not French, but you are English!? Then it is not der röte Kampfflieger or le Diable Rouge who keeps you awake at night! Instead, it is none other than the Red Baron!

Ratta tat, ratta tat, ratta tat! The sounds of my machine guns bore a hole in your dreams as you try try try to get away from my ratta tat ratta tat ratta tat!

Welcome to my digital journal here on the web!! Glad all of you, no matter what country you are from, were able to find your way here.

Of course, had you been FLYING in your mediocre machines to try and meet me, you would have little success as I would be hiding, there in the clouds, with my ratta tat ratta tat ratta tat (my machine guns), which would do you in! Will you become my 45th downed opponent!? Will you crawl home in defeat after meeting me face-to-face in the skies!? Know this, and know this well— der röte Kampffleiger will defeat you with little effort and take your lives in the process!!

Be sure to visit the sites of all those who have fallen to me—I have a helpful link list there to the right so that it's simple and easy to peruse their sites (which are hardly ever updated, due to the fact that they're DEAD!).—My doing, FYI.

I have, of course, provided this list to immortalize der röte Kampfflieger's triumphs! With each downed plane, I will include yet another link to their blogs! A way for you to see that each of my successes represents another's failure! Ratta-tat ratta-tat ratta-tat! (And because the supply of silver, which I used to use to create silver goblets memorializing each of my "kills," has recently been restricted here in Germany!)

But what does der röte Kampfflieger care about such trivial things! Do you see that list of forty-four links!? They have all fallen to the superior skills of le Diable Rouge! The, as you say with wonder, Red Baron!

Hope you've had such a wonderful time here on my blog! I will hope to update this again soon with more links to those who have fallen to my ratta-tat ratta-tat ratta-tat (machine guns)!!

Until then, you know who this is!

From: **http://www.lordbaden-powell.uk/scoutingblog/**

Subject: **Scouting for Boys**

Scrumptious, just simply scrumptious!

A jolly time was had in South Africa—if not the direct result of a successful campaign against the Zulus, but more importantly due to the smiling, cheery faces and attitudes of my personal team of native boys! My own personal team of native boys! Oh, how I love the sound of it. I immediately came back to the U.K., and rewrote my now best-selling book *Aids to Scouting* to incorporate all that I had learned by working so closely with my dark-skinned comrades!

While the scouting I required my toned friends to take part in—dreadful things like staying up at all hours (even though I'd sometimes spend the time with them because I am just that type of man) standing guard and, even worse, acting as a messenger to deliver notes across enemy lines . . . These young native men bonded together, looked out for each other, and were even there to lend a hand or a hug when things weren't looking so cheery! It was heartwarming to see, and even more disturbing when, while under my command, some of my beloved native friends were injured or killed! Simply dreadful!

Scouting, as I decided, should no longer be associated with violent conflicts—but should be colored by heartwarming, friendly camaraderie consisting of a young group of boys! No more standing up at all hours, working the body to maximum fatigue levels (well, in war that is)! The new scouting, as per ME, should be a cheery, happy, sunny experience for all! It was at that point when the "idea of the century" hit me!

Costumes. We must integrate costumes! The kind that make me want to just eat those little scouts up!

Being a scout is not about tracking a wild animal through the wilderness or building a fire per se—it is all about style! Yes, they should have neat little costumes with shiny fabrics and bandannas and patches that show off their unique little talents. They should wear emblems and knee-high socks and have learned a whole list of rollicking songs which they should also know the dance steps to! My scouts should find options when it comes to dressing up—not just one color or style. Give them the creative freedom to make their own styles and show them off to the rest of the young boys they share their time with. Aah, but will society . . . Will people really encourage their children to take part in such feel-good club activities?

I say YES. I say that there's nothing a father wants more than to see his young son take pride in his patches and his fabrics and his adorable little bandannas and his good deeds.

This thing is going to be huge, I can feeeeeel it!

From: **http://www.dianfossey.org/zaireblog/**
Subject: **My First Year with "Him"**

Girls, I am in LOVE.

I know I know I know! I've been horrible at keeping in touch, but this last year has been absolutely amazing! A year of growth, mutual understanding and true bonding with you know who. He's at my side 24/7 and, well, I am feeling a connection that I have never felt before with any of the others!

You would die! He is so affectionate and caring. So in touch with his emotions. We'll be out in the wilderness and he'll just play with my hair without me even having to ask him to. He's so playful, too—he loves whacking me with leaves and branches! It's funny, how cultural differences manifest themselves between two different creatures like he and I. I have to say, and don't quote me on this, but this is my first relationship where all that confusing miscommunication is gone! We are there, looking into each other's eyes, and we so GET each other. Hee! You can hear the excitement in just my words, can't you?

I have learned in the past that for a relationship to develop and move forward, someone must always give in to the other individual. Sure, it's a kind of social experiment if you really think about it, but I'm willing if it means that I'll find what I'm looking for. Oh, who am I kidding—I don't want there to be an end! I hope there never is. My time with him is one of the most valuable moments between sunup and sundown.

The other day he was sooooo cute. He vocalized his feelings to me, in such a way that I really can't even begin to try to communicate. It was this really sweet moment when he opened his mouth and told me exactly how he was feeling! I didn't even have to push him—it was all voluntary! Such a powerful communicator, if you ask me. Just amazing!

I've given him such a cute little nickname, "Digit," which he doesn't seem to mind at all. I think he likes it, too—unlike some of my other relationships, you can tell they just don't quite appreciate being given a nickname like that. Well, Digit loves it. Heh. He's sort of proud that I gave him a nickname, I think—it shows how we feel about each other.

Okay, I gotta go but I'll write more later. Seems that Digit and the rest of his brethren are going out to scavenge for food! I'm sure Digit will ask me to come along in his own, subtle way. That would be great—a real step forward in the relationship. I'll just have to make a conscious effort to not be overbearing or anything like that. You know how these guys get!

From: **http://www.cecil_b_demille.com/BLOG/**

Subject: **Official Announcement!!!**

Your world is about to CHANGE!!

Everything you know about BLOGGING will be USELESS!!

ARE YOU READING WHAT I HAVE TO SAY? CAN YOU EVEN IMAGINE WHAT IS COMING YOUR WAY!? A BLOG THE LIKES OF WHICH NO MERE MORTAL HAS EVER SEEN IS ABOUT TO CRUSH EVERYTHING ELSE AROUND YOU!

THE CECIL B. DEMILLE BLOG IS COMING SOON . . .

YES, there have been other blogs that have come before! YES! There are others who write journals! YES YES YES!!! Some of you may say that there are just too many of them out there for one more to matter!!

NO!

THE CECIL B. DEMILLE BLOG will bring forth the most SPECTACULAR blogging features EVER SEEN!

SEE OVER 1,000 NEW POSTS DAILY—ALL WRITTEN BY CECIL B. DEMILLE!

SEE OVER 1 MILLION COMMENTS DAILY—ALL WRITTEN BY CECIL B. DEMILLE!

SEE BILLIONS OF COLORS AND GRAPHICS—ALL CHOSEN BY CECIL B. DEMILLE!

SEE TRILLIONS OF LINKS!! GAJILLIONS OF TRACKBACKS! A GOOGLE OF FUN!

INTERACTIVE ELEMENTS **NEVER BEFORE SEEN OR EXPERIENCED!!**

YOU WILL MARVEL AT ITS AMAZING TECHNOLOGY!!
YOU WILL BE STUNNED BY ITS PROFESSIONAL DESIGN!!
YOU WILL LOSE YOUR BREATH AS YOU READ CECIL B. DEMILLE'S
GENIUS!!

AND IT WILL BE FREE! FREE! **FREE!**

DON'T MISS OUT!

DON'T BE THE LAST IN YOUR NEIGHBORHOOD TO EXPERIENCE THE
FULL-SPECTRUM EXPERIENCE THAT WILL BE THE CECIL B. DEMILLE
BLOG!

SIGN UP NOW FOR THE <u>MAILING LIST</u> SO YOU CAN BE THE FIRST IN
YOUR NEIGHBORHOOD TO VISIT THE GREATEST, BIGGEST, MOST POW-
ERFUL BLOG ON THE FACE OF THE ENTIRE EARTH!!*

*THE CECIL B. DEMILLE BLOG cannot confirm the fact that this blog is the most powerful blog on
the face of the earth.

From: **http://www.bonnieandclyde.com/blog/**
Subject: **Domain Name Acquisition!**

If you got an idea or a business but you don't got the domain name, you ain't never gonna make the dough. But through us, we can get you any domain name you want. Even if someone else already got it. Yes, that's right. Someone has what you want and they don't wanna give it to you? We'll make 'em give it to you. Trust us. Just look at some of the ones we already got, that we can give to you, for a very reasonable price:

www.herberthoover.com
www.fdr.com
www.cocacola.com
www.johnsmith.com
www.business.com
www.cars.com
www.alcatrazisland.com
www.alberteinstein.com
www.england.com
www.japan.com
www.unitedstates.com
www.thewhitehouse.com
www.wizardofoz.com

These are just some of the domains we can getcha. Do you wanna have a President's name for your domain? No problem. Want one that your neighbor already has and he ain't givin' it up? Drop us a note. Between the twos of us, we'll getcha what you want for very little up-front dough.

Also, once you get the site you want, you may find that you ain't got nuthin' to say. Well, look to us. We can provide you with a variety of already written blogs on topics that range from:

Science
Mathematics
Gravity
Hollywood
Technology

Foreign Relations
Romance
and
Radio Repair

If there's somethin' you want and you don't see it here, doesn't mean we can't get it. Just fill out our <u>request form</u> and we'll get back to you as soon as we find a place to hide out in.

From: **http://www.johnharvey_kellogg.edu/blog/**
Subject: **Day 7693, Battle Creek Sanitarium Philosophy #7,693**

Inspirational Health Thought #7693: Insanity is nothing more than the result of one's mistreatment of their bowels. [View the previous 7692 inspirational health thoughts.]

Here at the Battle Creek Sanitarium, I have had many dealings with people suffering from a myriad of ailments. Each one of them, cured by voluntarily joining my program of healthful activity, vegetarian lifestyle and high-fiber diet. It's what convinced my brother Will and I that the only way to give people the opportunity to heal themselves in the privacy of their own home was to start our own high-fiber cereal company. It's name? Sanitas Food Company.

Get it? San-itas? Sane? Get it? People who are **insane** will become sane after eating the whole grain goodness of San-itas products!

The names of the cereals, of course, have yet to be decided—but I have suggested at length to my brother that we must integrate the ideas of insane and ill individuals who have become healthy (i.e., reaching that point where they're suddenly and miraculously healed) into the names of the cereals!

In my 20+ years here at the Sanitarium, I have realized three things about those who are unable to control their mental or physical health. There comes a point, when they are given life-changing information about how to heal themselves—this is when they SNAP into reality. The knowledge that there is a solution to their previously insurmountable odds often gets them thinking, an electric CRACKLE of sorts shooting throughout their brains—and since the body is primarily an energy source, the idea of such a thing is not far from reality. When a subject experiences the first two steps of reaching a healthy lifestyle, they often POP to attention, and act on such things. These themes, of course, should be incorporated into the names of our products.

And so, I have suggested to Will that we incorporate the words "FIBER," "CORN" and possibly "BOWEL" into our first few cereals. Based on my experience and writings, I encouraged Will that we should move forward as quickly as possibly on our "Fiber Corn Bowel Breakfast Cereal," to which he seemed less than pleased.

We are working through a few issues right now, but I hope to resolve them before the week is up. Yes, Will is threatening to sever ties and start his own cereal company where he'd rather name his cereal something a little more "snappy," but I think that would be the biggest mistake in his entire life.

From: **http://mx.frida_kahlo.com/blog/**

Subject: **Desperate for Dumont**

I must be quick to thank all the generous readers who have sent their best of wishes and kindest of words to me—yes it seems as though Diego and I have hit what some may call a little bit of a rough patch in our marriage, but I do believe with *God* as my witness, that things will eventually come full circle. I've posted some of the wonderful wishes on my <u>Guest Book</u> for others to see.

But more importantly, I must share my excitement with everyone (especially the ladies) that I have been contacted to possibly become the spokesperson for the company they call <u>Dumont</u>. If you do not know, <u>Dumont</u> is a company located in none other than Switzerland, which has been making <u>tweezers</u> since 1875! And these are not any ordinary <u>tweezers</u>, not at all—these are high-quality, durable and detailed <u>tweezers</u> whose advanced engineering has resulted in a <u>tweezer</u> that can excavate the hardest of stubborn stubble! Trust me when I tell you I know about these things!

I use <u>Dumont's XL-87</u> tweezers every single morning, during lunchtime, and in the afternoon and evening as I clean up my well-known brow-line, shaping it with such ease. I often can be heard screaming "Dios Mío!" due to my excitement and pleasure in using such a well-created piece of equipment! Did you know that <u>Dumont</u> is the largest manufacturer of <u>tweezers</u> in the world? That they supply a wide variety of businesses through their vast national and international distribution network!?

Neither did I. And do you know what? Such details mean nothing to me!

But what DOES mean something to me, Frida Kahlo, is that my eyebrow hairs, which were at once unruly and hard to pull from my forehead (and even painful—ouch!), are no longer an issue now that I use the <u>Dumont XL-87</u> advanced tweezer technology! Now I can spend much more time concentrating on my paintings instead of having to labor for hours with a lesser-tweezer that just doesn't grasp my hairs in the way I hope that it would.

It is extremely premature for me to even be mentioning the <u>Dumont</u> product, or the fact that if you <u>click here now</u> you will get not only the <u>XL-87 tweezer</u> plus the complimentary brush kit and the click-on spotlighting system (for those dark bathrooms), but you will also get a wonderfully ornate silk carrying case just for buying this <u>amazing product</u>.

But don't take my word for it (I am just an innocent bystander singing the praises of the wonderful <u>Dumont product</u>)—check out these <u>pictures</u> of all the eyebrow hair I was able to pull out (these are full hairs, women, not broken pieces which lesser-tweezers often mangle)—I am looking right now into the mirror as I type this and can I just say that my single eyebrow looks so well manicured that I hope this whole agreement goes through with <u>Dumont</u> so I will never be without one of the most amazing products I have ever used.

I'm still working on my latest painting, *Self-Portrait with Monkey,* who personally, could really benefit from these tweezers as well!!

From: **http://www.williamhearst.com/blog**

Subject: **Top 10 Alternative Titles for Citizen Kane**

10. Citizen Bane of My Existence
09. Citizen Grain of Truth
08. Lies and the Lying Liars Who Tell Them
07. Citizen Stain on the Face of Society
06. Citizen Train Wreck of a Picture
05. Citizen Mainly Lies
04. Citizen Plain Ol' Crap
03. Citizen No-Fame, if I Have Anything to Do with It
02. Citizen Pain in My Ass
01. Citizen Lame, Yes You Are, Mr. Welles

I may not be a writer or a creative man, but if RKO likes any of these, they are more than welcome to borrow them while they are promoting the above film, which I have not seen.

Strangely, the *New York Daily Mirror*, the *Chicago Examiner*, the *Boston American, Cosmopolitan, Harper's Bazaar*, and the *International News Service* have all given this picture a bad review! I guess it might not be so good.

Heard some gossip about Orson Sells out? Send it to me here. We pay top dollar for good information as you may have already heard after we paid a small fortune for this picture of Orson Welles nude on a beach with a huge zucchini.

From: **http://www.ernest_shackleton.uk/blog/**
Subject: **Today's Thoughts on Name Changes**

Update: The *Endurance* has been trapped in an ice floe for over six months now. We have had many opportunities to push our way out and escape, but each has failed. It is a desperate time and I fear that the motivation and enthusiasm of the crew is suffering. We are desperate. Depressed. Fearful for our lives.

What do you think about me changing my last name?

When Adrien de Gerlache and Lars Christensen couldn't take delivery of their massive wooden ship the *Polaris*—it was offered to me. It was the perfect (NOT) ship for an expedition to the South Pole and I immediately purchased it for £11,600. The only step remaining was to change its name to the *Endurance*! Which, really, didn't have any real effect on its endurance, but it was a much better name than *Polaris*, which, to me, makes me think of the water UNDER the ice—and really, do you want to name a ship after the kind of water you hope to not be sinking in!? I think not!

This got me thinking about my name. Shackleton. Shackle. Shackles are that which keeps one secured against their will. This is not the kind of tone or theme I find that I'd like to communicate with my name. Secondly, by including the "ton" to the end of Shackleton, I get the feeling as if people might consider my name to refer to a "ton of Shackles" or more incarceration than anyone could ever imagine! Simply based on the current "incarcerated" and "shackled to the ice" situation we are in . . . Well, it's a bad idea. Every time someone says my name, you can see it on everyone's faces—thoughts of being "shackled" and "captured" and "kept against our will." At least, I can see it. I know they're thinking that. So I've suggested to them, let's change my name!

Some of my officers have told me I'm simply insane to change my last name—it is the name that is famous for reaching the southernmost point on the South Pole and that which garnered me a knighthood. But perhaps an alternative to Shackleton can illustrate something more freeing?

For what is the opposite of being shackled? It is having freedom to go anywhere, perhaps a tropical locale like the Hawaiian Islands, possibly Maui—which I am a big fan of. And the word "ton" should be something far less heavy-handed, like an ounce, or a cup, or something "tiny." Yes. YES.

Sir Ernest Henry Mauitiny. (pronounced: "mow-wee-tie-knee")

I think that should get the crew into a much more positive, less "feeling trapped" attitude. I'll update you tomorrow on how it went over!

From: **http://www.jimmyhoffa.se/moblog/**

Subject: **An Offer I Couldn't Refuse**

I been MIA for a few months now, s'why you haven't seen much pop up 'round here. But ol' Jimmy Hoffa's got more goin' on than ever before. The rumors of my disappearance have, in fact, all been wrong.

Back in July, I had myself a meetin' at the ol' Machus Red Fox joint in Bloomfield Hills. Was gonna meet up with "Tony Jack" and "Tony Pro" about certain Teamster issues as they related to their business and mine. Thing is, the boys don't show up and I'm sittin' around waitin' with my hand up my ass when a group of these little people stroll on into the joint.

Little people = dwarfs = midgets = circus performers, whatever the hell you wanna call 'em. The leader, who called himself Sir Geebley Faltskog, stepped forward and jumped up on the swingin' stool to shake my hand and announced that they were all from Sweden and most of 'em didn't even speak English but that they had come all the way for one of these meet-ups with the rest of their little friends. I didn't pay much attention at the beginning there until the little Geebley fella opens up a brief-case filled with cash and says there's more back in Sweden if I wanna come organize the whole Swedish dwarf population so theys can get paid a fair amount for all the tumblin' and jumpin' around they do over there.

Let's face it—things back in the States weren't as good as they used to be. With that attempted bribery conviction (which was overturned) and the whole Teamsters issue, who weren't listenin' to me as much as they used to (those shortsighted fools), I figured a change of scenery would do me some good. So I got into their bus, took a plane to Stockholm, Sweden, and I been here ever since.

In just the last few months I've organized almost 75% of all the "little people" (that's what you call 'em and if you call 'em anything else from this point forward I'll pop you one) here in Stockholm. From the tossin' kind to the pack 'em in a car kind to the kinds who dress up like clowns and entertain your stupid kids to the kinds who you seen in movies like *The Wizard of Oz*—not one part of the society over here is ever again gonna lowball these little guys for the big work they do. They got me to deal with now.

One thing that ain't no different . . . the bull and the horns. You try to offer less than a good fee for a midget party or try to lowball some dwarfs and you'll quickly find a city that has no little people willin' to do anything for nothin'.

So yeah, that's where I'm at. Hopefully, this info'll get the authorities to let up on the Tonys and Charlie O'Brien—who had nothing to do with me goin' missin'. Besides—I'm alive with the little people here, and I ain't never felt this big in my entire life!

Sorry, but you won't be able to contact me.

From: **http://www.aaronburr.com/blog/**

Subject: **What a Wednesday!**

Fate obviously hates one Aaron Burr. (That's me, in case you, you know, didn't know.)

First, good ol' friend Thomas Jefferson, who is quite obviously no longer my friend but seems to want to pretend he is my friend at social engagements, drops me from the ticket, thus removing any chance of my becoming his Vice President for yet another term. Thanks, buddy! Good luck to you. Really. Good luck. No, I'm serious. Good luck!

Then, my decision to run for Governor of New York, which it seems is the next best thing to becoming Vice President or President, is thwarted by none other than those horrible Clintons of New York. Thanks, guys! Really. No, thanks. You've really done wonders for my political career. Uh huh.

And lest we not forget the wonderful positive words being heaped upon my plate by one Alexander Hamilton, who has taken every public opportunity to speak ill about me—and for what? I have no idea. He just hates me. Apparently. For no reason. Which I find extremely depressing and confusing. Why why why why why!

So, yesterday (Wednesday), I arranged to meet the Hamilton-Hater in Weehawken to patch things up because I prefer to have people like me than hate me and anything I can do to make that happen I will, but you know what the wonderful orator brings with him? He brings guns. GUNS! And he says, *"why are you talking about me behind my back"* and I say, *"I'm not talking about you behind your back"* and he says, *"you are so talking about me behind my back and I don't like it"* and I say, *"you're living in a fantasy world Mr. Hamilton because I never have talked about you behind your back it was you who talked behind my back"* and he says, *"no, I was very public about my thoughts on you which makes it talking in front of your back which isn't the same as talking behind your back"* and I say *"that doesn't matter as much as why did you bring guns here today if you're a front-back talker instead of a back-back talker"* and he says *"because you wanted to duel me"* and I say *"I never said that"* and he says *"sure you did, you told me to get to the DUEL ON TIME"* and I say *"no I said that we should talk and resolve these issues in DUE TIME"* and he pauses and there's this long long long pause before he says, *"well while I'm here we might as well duel unless you're afraid that you'll lose"* to which I say, *"fine Mr. Hamilton let's duel but let history be aware of the fact that it wasn't my idea to duel"* to which Hamilton says, *"you better believe I'm going to make sure that history remembers today's events accurately—after I walk away from this place as the winner . . ."*

Well, I didn't have much else to say as Hamilton handed me the gun . . . I was none too pleased, primarily due to the negative atmosphere all around me. And we line up and we shoot our guns and what do you expect but Hamilton is a horrible shot and hits a tree branch while my gun, which I shot with my eyes closed, ends up shooting him above his right hip. I'm thinking ohmygodohmygodohmygod, I just shot Hamilton.

So, yeah. Yesterday wasn't really that great of a day and I hope that things are better today and tomorrow. Waiting to hear if Hamilton is okay—which I hope he is, 'cause if he isn't, that's gonna sort of ruin today and the rest of the week as well and add to a pretty depressing year of horrible events that fate has decided to heap upon my plate.

Fate! I curse you!

From: **http://www.plato.gr/blog/**

Subject: **Today's Blogalogue!**

So, yeah—let's blogalogue!

What is UP with the Universe these days? Hmm? Like, we can see it but we can't. We know it's there but we can't prove it. It surrounds us, yet we do not feel it. It's like a bowl of fruit sitting on a table—that you can see, that you can describe, that you can talk about—but which you can't taste! Well, at least around my parts you can't taste it or you end up getting your hand slapped! Ha! Seriously, folks—explain THAT one to me!

Or what about wisdom? What is UP with wisdom these days? Everyone thinks they have it, yet it's those who think they have it who don't have it at all! And those who don't think they have it and strive to find it end up already having it! It makes my brain twist up in knots just thinking about it! Seriously, can you even comprehend it? No? Maybe that means you don't have any wisdom at all! Oh, I'm just kiddddding!!!

Oh boy, the other day I was out in the courtyard of the Academy where I teach and I witnessed two students debating moderation. While they debated, they continued to stuff their faces with food! Do you HEAR what I'm saying!? Can you even IMAGINE? What is UP with that!? And yet, while moderation has nothing to do specifically with one's consumption of food it encompasses the consumption of every resource around us, whether that be food, knowledge, respect, love, wisdom or justice! Or even politics!

Hooooo boy. Did I just mention politics!? No groaning here. Well, okay groan if you want. But seriously, why do politicians tell you ONE THING and do something completely different? Why does government ask for your input then never use it to better society!? Why are those in power always losing their hair!? You wanna know why, I'll tell you why! Because only philosophers, with our long curly thick hair, are fit to rule. You remember Samson!? What happened to that guy when he lost his hair? He lost his power! Ladies—listen up! Don't you cut your husband's hair if you want him to be successful. Please! Don't get me started on that . . .

And what about courage!? That's right, COURAGE. What is up with courage these days? Nobody seems to have it. They have AGE, sure. But cour-AGE? Seems that we can't have everything we want in life, except life itself!

Okay—I must get back to my cave! Haha, yes—the one with the shadows in it! Shadows! What is up with SHADOWS!? They're there but they're not really there!? It's enough to make your mind twist up in knots!

From: **http://www.samuel_morse.com/blog/**

Subject: •••• ••

From: **http://www.bob_marley.com/dablog/**

Subject: **Dontcha Worry . . .**

A serious t'ing happened, mon. I and the bredren were red, ya? Da spliff be passin' 'round t'a room . . . Good times, mon. Gooooood times. Den 'fore we see it, more red 'n' just our heads. Da bushes up in flames, smokin', cracklin'. Rasta try 'n' put out every little than' but da spliffs burn up, mon—so do all da happy bushes . . .

Sad, sad times . . . I, the Wailers, the Rasta—how we gonna get red without no supply?

Da bredren, da sistren—Ites is gone, now da red and da spliffs and the massive supply o' what the Rasta 'ave, all gone. No danks to da polytricks 'ere in this wonderful set o' states—Rasta all out of cannabis and Bob Marley needs all da help from 'is Rastafari bredren 'n' sistren.

They's speakin' an sayin' dere places 'round 'ere, which da Rasta know. Like little birds singin' their t'ing . . . tellin' Rastafari ta don' worry 'bout a thin' that ev'ry little thin's gonna be 'right.

A wha' dem seh?

I bredren hear the little birds singin' their t'ing. Don' worry 'bout a thin'.

A wha' dem seh? I and I shoot out <u>da message</u> through da digital post—get out da word that I and I bredren in desprat need . . . Desprat and da bredren is gettin' more normal by da secon'.

Den by da door, a sound 'n' I and I bredren open it and da friends of da Rasta standin' dere. Holdin' spliffs. My spirit rise to da Ites, so too for da sistren. Sure, mon, da polytricks and da laws of dis here place no good for da Rastafari but I and I bredren don' much matter, don' much care. For, when da little bird singin' their t'ing—and tellin' I and I bredren don' worry . . . I and I bredren don' worry. We smoke da spliffs and play da music and dats just what I and I bredren gonna do.

Ya, mon. I and I love this digital world. Even wit da downgression and downpression, I and I know dat da spliffs, theys I and I t'ing. Ya. Feeeeelin' good, mon.

Don' worry. No way.

From: **http://www.wilbur_wright.com/flying_blog/**

Subject: **Master Pilot, Wilbur Wright!**

Yesterday was the day. Earlier this year, due to some very unique thinking on my part, I was able to include my brother Orville in the building of the *Wright Flyer* (picture here). Following our glider flights, this was to be the very first machine with a propeller (carved) and a fully functioning engine.

Thanks to Charlie Taylor, who helped me in building the engine, I then decided to move forward in filing for patents and whatnot, making the *Flyer I* (I decided the name change would be a good idea because we'd probably have more than one Wright-sponsored flying aeroplane) its final name.

Testing, which I coordinated and organized over the course of many months, showed that the engine was working almost perfectly—it was unfortunately not operating at 100%, but with a few quick adjustments (some of which I suggested to Charlie after really putting my brain to work) brought it up to 80% and which resulted in it being the best of any previous engines we'd put together. One of the great ideas I came up with involved using a bicycle chain in the engine—just wildly deciding to use things from around the shop! Again, an inspired choice—it worked flawlessly. The next step was to test out the *Flyer I* and see if my vision of men in the air would actually come true. Oh, and I invited Orville to come along as well—although I told him that if he was going to get all whiny like he usually did that he should stay home. He, of course, being the annoying little brother he is, decided that he had to be there.

So yesterday, December 17, 1903, was the day.

Let me just explain something here. A first flight is always dangerous. There's always the chance of getting injured or possibly killed. As my brain was filled with all the technical specifications and the solutions to any design or engine problems, I needed to find someone willing to put their life at risk for the first flight. After Charlie refused I was able to force Orville to do so. With my help, and the aeroplane, he was able to successfully stay at 120 feet for about 12 seconds.

I immediately took to the air, following my successful first flight (with pilot Orville at the helm) and surpassed his flight by staying up for 59 seconds at a height of 852 meters. That's right! Higher, longer and better than Orville. You could tell he was a bit upset, but I'm sure he'll get over it.

Whatever you do, don't rub it in his face. He doesn't even know I write my thoughts here, so keep it quiet. In the meantime, here are pictures of me flying.

Congratulatory messages should be sent to me, here.

From: **http://www.orville_wright.com/flying_blog/**

Subject: **I Believed We Could Fly, and We Did!**

You can call me Mister Orville Wright!

I'm sure you've heard the news by now—even though some of the papers (the small ones) either didn't report it or got it wrong . . . Yesterday was my first official flight on the *Flyer I* (a homage to the nickname my parents gave me as a kid—I used to fly around everywhere and I was the "little one"— thus, *Flyer I* (One)). Following those boring glider trips—this one was packed with a little something that Charlie Taylor and I thought up . . . an engine that we got running to about 90% capacity.

You can imagine how big brother Wilbur tried to take credit for it—he goes around trying to convince people it was his idea, but Charlie and I just laugh about it behind his back. He wanted to call the plane the *Wright Flyer* (stuuuuupid!) until I reminded him that he might want to think about the future. What happens if we build another one? What do we call that? *The Wright Flyer II*? Wouldn't make sense. Gotta number these babies from the beginning. Wilbur finally caved—he knew who was right.

There was another point when stubborn Wilbur almost ruined the whole project—we couldn't get a normal chain working in the prototype engine . . . It just was too heavy, weighing down the aeroplane. So, I'm sitting there in the bicycle shop working on a bicycle and I turn to the guys and I say, "What about a bicycle chain?" Well, Wilbur was quick to say no because he just likes to say no, but when Charlie played around with it for a while, he realized that my idea was gold. Wilbur didn't like that either.

That's why I was so surprised and honored that he chose me to fly the plane yesterday for the first time. I mean, that was so nice for him to do, he didn't have to. I mean, he is the older brother. But he said to me, "Orville—you have worked so hard over all these months and I want you to have the chance to fly the *Flyer I* first. You deserve it more than I do." Man, I thought that was so great of him to say, and you'd better believe that I jumped at the chance.

I stayed up in the air for about 12 seconds at 120 feet. They even took pictures of me doing it. When I got back down, you could tell that Wilbur was a bit upset about the fact, but I'm sure he'll get over it.

Whatever you do, don't rub it in his face. He doesn't even know I write my thoughts here, so keep it quiet. In the meantime, here are <u>pictures of me flying</u>.

No more notes, okay? I'm just glad that we've taken such a big step in the world of flight!

From: **http://www.alexander_graham_bell.com/blog/**

Subject: **Hello? Are you there!?**

Hahaha. Get it? I invented the telephone. See? Ha! Inventors and scientists can be funny!!

Thanks for visiting the official blog of Alexander Graham Bell! Unlike some of those other stuffy inventors and scientists (ahem, Thomas Edison's phonograph blog and Melville Bissell's carpet sweeper blog immediately come to mind as useless boring drivel) who have their assistants transcribe their thoughts and notes to their pages, I write each and every thing on here all by my lonesome! And yes, it is lonesome! Haha! Get it? 'Cause I do it by myself and that's a solitary activity and— Yeah, okay.

I've got a brand-new project to introduce and I think you'll be really excited to hear about it! Heh! (Get it? One of my inventions is dependent on being able to hear!! Heh.) You may or may not know that before I ever invented the telephone, I figured out a way to send piano music electronically over long distances! Well, now that I've invented the telephone, I'm combining that with the music element to introduce to you . . .

Alexander Graham Bell's Telephone Ringtones!

Just click on any of the below musical pieces and they will be immediately sent to your home telephone! For free! In a sense, you're helping me troubleshoot a brand-new exciting feature for the home communications device!

But a word of caution—as this is still an experimental technology and because it requires the use of electricity to conduct the music . . . Pick up the phone with a glove on or something, okay? Hah! Kidding. You don't need a glove. But just don't put the phone to your ear . . . Go ahead and click on one and it should arrive in under 72 hours!

"I'll Take You Home Again, Kathleen" by Thomas Payne Westendorf
"Grandfather's Clock" by Henry Clay Work
"The Bonnie Banks o' Loch Lomond" by Andrew Lang
"Gay as a Lark" by Septimus Winner
"Old Aunt Jemima" by James Grace
"Symphony No. 1" by Johannes Brahms

"String Quartet No. 1" by Bedrich Smetana
"Old Macdonald" by Unknown
"Hello, are you there?" by Alexander Graham Bell
"Hi, it's me Alexander" by Alexander Graham Bell
"Answer the phone, already" by Alexander Graham Bell

Any problems, injuries, annoyances? E-mail <u>Thomas Edison</u>.

From: **http://www.judy_garland.com/blog/**

Subject: **Hi. HI. A89h*((7 !! !!**

Cheeeeeeeeeeeeeeeeeeeeeeeeeeeeeeeeeeeeeeeeeeeeeeese.

Look. Look at the cheese. No, not real cheese but the word cheese can you see it up there right above I just typed it out there for you here it is again cheeeeeeeeeeeeeeeeeeeeeeeeeeeeeeeeeeeeeeeeeeeeeeeeeeeeeeeeeeeeeeeeeeeeeeeeeese! Djal;8d

Lotsa cheeeeeeese. Cheese isn't a word, no it's not don't tell me it isn't 'cause it is and I can see it but it doesn't soudnaa t d,. doesnj't sound like cheese but cheese doesn't make a sound in the forest if you hit it with a axe or yes, I do.

I like vodka . . . aaand you do too or blue coo coo chee foo.

Cheeeese is yellow and yellow brick road with all those midgets they freak me out those little freaky small hand people when I was in trhe dressing room getting ready that day they came in accidental and didn't say what they wanted and I was changing and turned aournd and there they were, those little peopole wanting to say hello and I didni't want them there so I threw a glass or something and then when I was suppoed to be sing follow the yellow bric road they had mean looks on their faces which I can see now if I close my eyes and it's not really the memory but the thought that counts and if you dn't agree theyn you might as well just shut THE HELL UP BEDAUSAE I DON'T CARE WHAT YOU THINK ABOUTANYTHING ASSSSSSSSSSS.

;ADLI-89DHFS(SD*a98aud-&7&&897 sdyf9870-

rh4978\

2-r3998

(*(Sh;ks

Y&*D

That feel nice I'm gonna just rest my head down here and yeah until later so goin nighgt night talk to you soon tomorrow I'll post more.

*(&u7h98sdun

From: **http://www.moe_howard.com/blog/**

Subject: **I Hate Him**

Someone stole my bike today. I locked it up outside the house and did everything Dad told me to do but still someone got it. I didn't want to tell Dad 'cause he told me that I should lock it up behind the house but I was just going inside for a second and I didn't think anyone in the day would try to take it. When Dad came home I told him and he was really mad and pulled out the belt which I said No to. Then Dad said well if you don't want the belt then you're gonna be punished another way and I didn't even have warning and he poked me hard with two fingers in the eyes.

It really hurt bad and he said that he had to teach me a lesson and tried to do it again but I was smart that time and I held up my hand so his two fingers couldn't get me—but then he showed me his fist, just hangin' there in midair . . . He hit it with another hand, and he wound the fist in midair before hitting me on the head with it. I just started crying and then he slapped me and Curly ran into the other room so he wouldn't get slapped and Dad just said again how he wasn't buying me another bike until I could treat things with respect.

I hate him I hate him I hate him.

When I grow up and I have kids I ain't never gonna hit them or yell at them or poke them or nothin' like that. 'Cause it doesn't make a kid feel good or happy and it ain't funny or anything like that. Curly said the same thing, he said it's wrong and Dad should know that pokin' his kids ain't gonna do nothing but make them not like him.

And I say yes to that—when I grow up I ain't gonna be like him if it's the last thing I do.

From: **http://www.mecca.org/~muhammad_blog/**
Subject: **A Break from It All?**

These freakin' kids are driving me crazy.

First Fatimah wanted to hear stories. Now, I got crap to do and I tell Fatimah that, but she throws herself to the floor and starts screaming over and over again. I turn to Khadija and tell her that these are **her kids** and can she please get Fatimah to stop screaming, to which she just gives me "that look." Ugh. So what do I do? Yes, once again I sit down with Fatimah, tell her the one about the hummingbird poking holes in the blanket of the skies, thus forming the stars. It's a long one . . . but you can read it <u>here</u> if you care one bit.

So, right, back to the screaming Fatimah. She calms down. I sit down and try to just have a little time to myself when Zainab and Ruqayah start pulling me in both directions. They want to hide and have me find 'em. So I tell 'em to go hide, figuring I'll have a good few hours to relax. Before long, here comes Khadija again, now railing on me for leaving the girls unattended. Khadija, of course, has Umm Kulthum in her arms and unloads all the girls at my feet. She says something, which I don't pay much attention to, while the girls turn me into a donkey ride.

This is a house of estrogen, if you ask me. Sanity is running at an all-time low.

When the whole donkey ride storytime crap ended, I pulled Khadija aside and told her I had to get some quiet time to myself or I was going to literally explode. After getting roped into watching the girls for the next few days, I was able to eke out a night for myself . . .

It's like I'm a prisoner just trying to escape!

Either way, I got my time off. Tomorrow night. I'm gonna go out to that area near Mecca with all the caves—maybe some meditation and thought will do me some good. I just want some quiet time. No screaming kids, no pulling at my arms and legs, no responsibility.

No more voices!! That's what I want. Total and complete serenity. May I hear nothing but only the sound of my breath and the wind against the land. No more voices.

Aaah, if I can get that—I will be completely satisfied.

From: **http://www.julia_child.fr/foodblog/**
Subject: **The Tuna Sandwich**

I must admit, albeit somewhat embarrassed, but last night I was introduced to a meal they call "a tuna fish sandwich with chips on the side."

Dear readers, have you ever tried such a thing?

Housed in between two glorious slices of something they call "Wonder Bread" (most likely due to the wondrous taste sensation provided to one's taste buds by the spongy white goodness which elicits a wonderful "wow" from the eater) was a simply spectacular lump of a fish they find deep in the ocean referred to simply as "tuna." The texture, both disturbing and strange all at once, is in fact—a taste sensation when combined with a heaping cup of mayonnaise. But even more spectacular was the way in which the "side of chips" (potato, not fish as the English refer to their cod) was integrated into the meal. Instead of eating them as if they were separate from the entire concoction—the chips were mashed and crunched into a thousand tiny salty pieces and thrown in between the glorious Wonder Bread, in and among the smooth and silky mayonnaise-lathered tuna . . . Together, it was a glory that I can honestly say is second to none.

For dessert, as if I even expected anything to top the first and only course of this unique meal, was a sweet, spongy rod of heaven called the Winky. What winking has to do with this sweet treat I have no idea except for the fact that quite possibly only those who know the amazing nature of this treat will "wink" to others who have experienced such a thing, keeping those like yours truly (until yesterday) out of the secret Winky club. I must say, I shoved that golden cake filled with white opaque frosting into my mouth as quickly as I could—I'm sure I said something to my husband, Paul, about it but he couldn't hear a word at all. My mouth was filled to the brim with the goodness of the Winky.

Have you, dear readers, experienced such extraordinary food goodness? I have, it seems, been so caught up in introducing the American public to the recipes and foods of France that I have overlooked these two wonderful items of culinary perfection. Two items that I suspect are going to shape my career and my television program.

Long live the Winky! Long live the Winky!

This is Julia, saying toodles for now . . . As always, if you have a recipe you think the public may fancy, feel free to <u>contact me</u> and submit your meal.

From: **http://www.nikola_tesla.com/radioblog/**

Subject: **Radioblog #15**

This week's radioblog is now available <u>here</u> for download. Select transcripts from Tesla's radioblog #15 (featuring his good friend <u>Mark Twain</u>) can be read below:

--

{snip!}

Announcer: *"Broadcasting wireless from his Houston Street laboratory in New York, transforming his powerful radio signals via his amazing Tesla coils—it's Nikola Tesla with his special guest Mark Twain!!"*

[Farting sound]

Tesla: *"That's what I think of Marconi. A big smelly bag of wind!"*
Twain: *"You mean, Mar-phony, right, Tesla!?"*
Tesla: *"I invented radio. I pioneered it. Without the Tesla oscillator no one would even be trying to broadcast wireless radio signals! Marconi is a copycat, and by him trying to get his own patents for wireless signal technology—it's just stupid. He's an impostor!"*
Twain: *"Marconi, the phony!"*

[Laughter in the background]

Tesla: *"Show me someone out there broadcasting wireless signals and then ask them how they did it. Me. Me me me me me. Anyone who says they came up with it on their own is a total liar! LIAR! And yet people are out there listening to them, hearing them say they came up with radio, without any knowledge that it was me who did it in the first place. It makes me ill, really."*
Twain: *"Some people are without sense, Tesla. Don't worry about what they think."*
Tesla: *"You hear about that Edison fella?"*
Twain: *"Another copycat?"*
Tesla: *"I don't get it. It pisses me off. There would be NO RADIO if it wasn't for me. I am the KING OF ALL MEDIA! Yet all these people go around pretending it was them. Copying my act. It's not all about me either, I'd just like people out there to know that what they're hearing originated with me. I mean, if someone copied your crap—"*
Twain: *"Crap?"*

Tesla: *"You know what I mean . . . You'd want the world to know if someone started writing Tom Sawyer books and passing them off as their own, right?"*
Twain: *"Oh yeah. That would make me mad."*

[Woman's voice, screaming]

Tesla: *"Okay. We'll be back with some of the local ladies coming by to talk to Mark and myself after this little homage to my brand-new pal, Marconi the phony, and the love of his life."*
Twain: *"That's right—now it's time for . . ."*

Announcer [with booming voice]: *"MARCONI and EDISON: Stupid and Stupider!"*

{snip!}

For previous Tesla radioblogs, visit the Tesla Radioblog Archives. To visit the live show or see the Tesla coils firsthand, send an e-mail to Nikola.

From: **http://www.davy_crockett.com/blog/**

Subject: **The Alamo**

Can't write much.
Mexican forces number in the thousands.
Defending. Fighting. Protecting.

Whether or not we are successful in our defense of the Alamo mission, history must
never forget this moment in time. A cry or saying of some kind must help those over
the years remember. A rallying cry that will whip others into a frenzy in times of war
and strife . . .

I am not necessarily a wordsmith, but I have a few suggestions which I look to you to
help spread:

"Don't Forget This Here Place!"
"'Member the Mission!"
"This Here Place, There's No Forgettin' It!"
"The Ala-moans Were Numerous, the Sacrifice High."
"Remember What Happened at This Here Mission, Do You Hear?!"
"People Died There, Oh Yes It's True!"
"Be Mindful of the Mission!"
"Remember David Crockett—He Was There Too, You Know."

That's all I can write now.
My hope is to help thwart this surge of soldiers.
If I do not come out of this alive, do not forget my contributions to government and
Texas.

"Ala-No no no no no!"

That one's pretty good if you ask me.

From: **http://www.in.buddha.com/blog/**

Subject: **An Open Letter to Father**

I just want to come back home to the palace, Father. Pleeeeasssssee!

I know. I know I came across the "four sights"—the old crippled man and the diseased man and the decaying corpse and the ascetic, humorless individual. I know, I know, I know how I said living a life of riches was useless to me. I know how I said that the pleasures and wealth meant nothing to me. I know how I left my wife and my family behind for this life of being a monk . . .

But . . . well . . . people make mistakes, right? Sometimes? And then, even though they made a mistake, their parents who love them so much turn a blind eye to the mistake that was made. Right?

Please please please please please please please please please please please please thirteen hundred more times please!! Do not keep the doors of the palace off limits to me. Open the doors and your heart to your son Gautama! Seriously. C'mon. Open open open open open. I'm begging you. It's not as easy out here on my own as I thought it would be.

I have no attendants like Channa waiting on me, providing for me, making sure anything I need is ready at my first thought of it. I have no financial support. I will become a decaying corpse myself if you don't help me out and soon!

People say things they don't mean. When I said that the palace was a festering plot of gluttony, I wasn't necessarily talking about you, Father. I was just sort of, you know, playing around. A joke! You know? And when I called you the overlord of societal decay I meant that in the best of ways. I meant, you know, that you were so far over, or above trivial things like that. And when I said that the soul was blackened with a world of suffering—it was more like a metaphor . . . You know?

Not to mention, these monk robes? They rub the wrong way against my legs and give me rashes. I can hardly take three steps without feeling the burn.

Tell my wife, Yashodhara, that I miss her and want to come home to the palace! Tell her I have tried to send her messages but they have bounced back, unread, the same as my messages to you. You have left me no choice but to put my open letter to you, Father, here—where the rest of the world must see how much I regret my decision.

Can I come home now? Please?

From: **http://www.jules_verne.fr/futureblog/**

Subject: **A League of Their Own**

You enjoyed *20,000 Leagues Under the Sea*.

You reveled in the amazing journey as led by the gruff and adamant Captain Nemo! You gripped your book in fear as the gigantic squid attacked the fortified *Nautilus* submarine! Your eyes opened wide as you glimpsed, for the very first time, the lost city of Atlantis!!

But that was just the beginning!!

Due to popular demand, I have decided to bring the next chapter of the Captain Nemo saga to bookstores everywhere. As we speak, I am drafting the follow-up book to the amazing underwater adventure! People have said to me recently, including my well-respected colleagues, that it is a tough story to tell. What could possibly be different from the previous story? Sure, some have suggested it be in outer space or high above in the skies! But more underwater, they grumble! What will be so different that we will want to come back and read more?

This one goes to 21,000.

The sequel to my book will be called *21,000 Leagues Under the Sea*! There will be one full extra league of excitement! There will be one more league of mystery! And a league is a lot of extra story landscape—it is, in actuality, 5.56 kilometers! That is 5.56 more kilometers of adventure, drama, sea creatures and treasure!

Yes, your favorite characters will return! Yes, the darkness of the earth's oceans will open up as it did before. But now, there will be **3 more nautical miles** of nail-biting tension. **3 more nautical miles** of romance and heroism. **3 more nautical miles** of story!

Nautilus will no longer just go 20,000 leagues under the sea. This time, it'll go 21,000 leagues!

I am, of course, still rolling the idea around in my head, but what use is a digital diary if not to poll those who are fans of your work. So, if you have any thoughts about this idea (or <u>yesterday's</u> about *Around the World in 82 Days*) please send a message to <u>jules@jules_verne.fr</u>.

From: **http://www.lumierebrothers.fr/cinema-blog/**

Subject: **Premiere of the Cinématographe!**

If you're looking at this page, you have most likely heard of the Lumière Brothers and our amazing invention called, in French, the "Cinématographe"! An amazing new type of entertainment and technology, the Cinématograph projects moving images on a screen in a darkened room that makes you feel as if you are right there witnessing the action!! This December 28 will mark the World Premiere of our Amazing Films!

[Buy tickets here for the Blockbuster Premiere of the Cinématograph!]

If you are looking for particular starting times of particular Lumière Brothers film attractions, just click on the name of the film you would like to view and you will be presented with additional information!

On December 28, the Lumière Brothers will be proud to present these amazing, never-before-seen, must-see-event films:

—-

Arrival of a Train!   <u>BUY TICKETS</u>
The most amazing action picture ever produced!! There is a train coming straight toward the audience and what will they do!? It's coming closer!? Here, you'll wet your pants when you see a train coming right for you when, in fact, it's just another one of the Lumière Brothers films!

Baby's Lunch   <u>BUY TICKETS</u>
A baby is given lunch, and you are there to feel the stress! Watch in awe as the baby doesn't eat everything the mother wants to give him! A slapstick comedy in the vein of, well, nothing ever before seen!

The Sprinkler Sprinkled   <u>BUY TICKETS</u>
The comedy follow-up to the successful "Baby's Lunch," this lap-smacking farce is about a man and a sprinkler and the silly damp relationship the two share! Bring your bathing suits, you may just get wet!

Girl Opens Door   <u>BUY TICKETS</u>
A girl opens a door. Over and over again. Marvel as she opens that door right in front of your eyes. It will seem as though you're there opening the door too! A knee-slapping comedy tour de force!

Man Lights Candle   <u>BUY TICKETS</u>
In this mystery film, a man takes out a dangerous flame and lights a candle right before your eyes. It is as if the candle is right there, lighting up the darkness around you! How is it possible!? Then, he lights a candle over and over again! Amazing!

Woman Up Stairs / Woman Down Stairs (Double Feature)   <u>BUY TICKETS</u>
A film for the ladies! A woman goes up some stairs, and you feel as if you're right there with her! Then, she'll do it again and again and again! But wait, there's more! Here, in this double feature, you'll also get to see the same woman go down some stairs. Again and again. Stunning, a must-see!!

The Lumière Brothers pride themselves on their cutting-edge, must-see-event films! To subscribe to the Lumière Brothers mailing list and hear about our upcoming films, please send an e-mail <u>here</u>.

From: **http://www.leo_tolstoy.ru/blog/**

Subject: **Peace, Not War**

I have recently begun corresponding with a young Indian named Mohandas Gandhi—whose words you can read <u>here</u>. He is a young activist who shares my thoughts and feelings regarding war and pacifism and does so on his <u>blog</u> as well (although I find his comments to be awfully terse—I am able to finish reading his daily thoughts in a few short minutes). Although I have no way of knowing what impact this Gandhi figure may have on India in the long run, I am always pleased to share thoughts regarding the issues that matter to me while bridging the gap between language, culture and society. (I would suggest to him, had I known him better, that his name is not easy to spell and may not roll off the tongue as well as he may wish it to. A possible name change may work wonders for him.)

My most recent thoughts on societal evil can be found <u>here</u>. As these writings exceed 145 digital pages of text, I am unable to provide them for you here on the front page of my digital journal.

My supplemental thoughts on previous thoughts I had regarding the meshing of real historical figures with fictitious characters in my novel *War and Peace* can also not be presented here on this front page, as their pages number 243. Due to the length of this journal post you must <u>download it</u> and attempt to read it using your own mechanisms. Since I have written it I have been unable to reread it myself, due to the fact that any and all of my devices are unable to retrieve a file this large. What I can tell you, however, is it is impressively long!

I received some correspondence from those who read <u>www.leo_tolstoy.ru</u> who mentioned that my article entitled "The Positives of Peaceful Protest" had no text below the header. This was, it turns out, due to the fact that this article in particular was 452 pages long with a 10 point font. This comes out to be about 673 hand-written or typefaced pages and it appears as if the current technology cannot handle such a thing. I will attempt to post the shortened version, which comes in at around 259 pages—a quick read compared to the latter.

I have additional links to additional pieces that I have written for your perusal, but unfortunately, it appears as if those additional mentions ended up taking approximately 320 pages—which I can also not provide here on this front page due to loading issues. It appears as if I may have to break up the document, which includes links to all my documents and writings into shorter documents like today's text. In doing so, it will take me 1,298 days in which to communicate this information, but the information and links will then, at least, be available to you. Expect such information over the next three or more years.

If there's an article or document you are desperate to study, please do not hesitate to provide your contact information to <u>me</u>.

From: **http://www.ed_wood.com/blog/**

From: **http://www.gene_roddenberry.com/blog/**
Subject: **The Pitch!**

Today I pitched my one-hour sci-fi/action/adventure drama, *Star Trek*, to the network.

The pitch was solid, I think. I mean, I think it was solid. Damn, I'm not so sure. I know that when I mentioned the "wagon train" concept—you know, even though it's in space it's still about people riding around and stopping at different planets (i.e., towns) where stories unfold—I think I saw some nodding. Of course, there was no recognition from the network executives when I spouted out my astronomy equation about how many carbon-based life-forms there probably are in our galaxy.

2,800,000,000,000,000,000,000,000,000. (More on this equation here.)

They asked what that had to do with *Star Trek*!

The more I think about it, the more I can't quite tell how it went over. When I talked about the Captain (Robert M. April) I sensed that they were . . . Oh, who am I kidding! I didn't sense a thing. Wagon train. They got wagon train. Someone actually asked if there would be horses. HORSES! I may have even said, *"yes, there will be horses."* I don't even know anymore. Hell, if horses would get the show sold, I would include horses. Do you want horses!? You got 'em! (I could probably just let the crew go back to some kind of "alternate universe" where they could exist in scenarios that took place in familiar Earth settings like the Old West or 1920s Chicago or something . . .)

Who am I kidding? Maybe I should go back to being a cop!

When I mentioned the name of their ship, the SS *Yorktown*, I sensed that people didn't like it. I thought it was a good name. Strong, dedicated, powerful! The YORKTOWN!

I'm a total fraud, aren't I?

If I could have one wish right now it would be that in addition to selling this damn TV show, I would have no emotional attach-ment to it whatsoever. No emotions! At least then, no matter what happened, I could react to the situation with a calm, col-lected state of mind. Hmm. No emotions would save me from being sad, angry, frustrated, conflicted—all my downfalls! It's sort of a great idea for a character trait.

Oh, give it up, Roddenberry! That's the stupidest idea ever.

I'll post as soon as I know what happens—for all THREE of you who happen to have stumbled across this site by accident. (Not you, Mother.)

From: **http://www.albert_einstein.org/blog/**
Subject: **Staggering Frustration . . .**

About five or six weeks ago I took my usual break from the patent office to take a stroll around the outskirts of the city with my good friend Michele Besso—you may recall my <u>writings</u> from weeks ago (one of my few posts on this very complicated blog software)—my head was weighed down with a thousand thoughts about a thousand ideas and I was attempting to find the connective tissue between all of them. Michele is, indeed, so sharp and patient at the same time that he allows my words to simply hang out there for seconds, sometimes minutes at a time—sometimes they connect and sometimes they do not.

This particular time . . . they did.

I went home that night still close to what I was striving for but not fully grasping that which I had been looking for until the following morning. The excitement was palpable. This theory of relativity was more concrete than ever before. Finally, people who showed me no respect or consideration in the past would see that I had something worthwhile to contribute. I immediately set out to put these theories to the digital page so that there would be no delay, the kinds which normal ancient paper presses are ruled by. I would write them and print them here for the whole world to see!

There was one tiny impasse.

That impasse is this device which I have yet to fully grasp (which scares me every time I share a look with its blank, dark screen). I visited my neighbors—their son, at a ripe age of ten, knows more about operating this machine and the software within it than I can ever hope to know. He instructed me again as to how I could put my thoughts here on the digital page for all to see. After hours of explanation and reexplanation (really, one must need to be a genius in order to operate one of these marvels), I felt comfortable enough to begin writing straight into the blog's interface.

There was my viewpoint on the production and transformation of light. My thoughts on the kinetic theory of heat. Theories on electrodynamics of moving bodies and my special theory of relativity. Six weeks and thirty pages of work. I hit SUBMIT and waited.

And waited. And waited. There was a beep of some kind, then a strange error message popped up in front of me. I turned the power button off and on again, in the hopes that it would fix the problem. Yet, when it came back on, everything I had written was gone.

The screen was blank.

Gone. It had disappeared! Everything. I frantically fetched the neighbor's son, who searched but to no avail. Important documents, I told him. Life-changing theories!! He had to retrieve them, all this work I had done.

The child looked to me and in an almost innocent voice exclaimed that he was, indeed, no genius. Indeed.

Of course, this text appears with no problem! There is no rhyme or reason to the odds involved with such a confounding situation.

I stare at the blank screen now with despair. The thoughts are still in my head, albeit a little less coherent, but I fear having to do it all over again and things are busy at the patent office as usual. I will see if my motivation comes back in a few weeks and possibly try again.

Ugh. I just don't get these computers. Too confusing. My mind . . . it just can't grasp it.

From: **http://www.cleopatra.com/blog/**

Subject: **Vacationing to Rome!**

44 B.C. is so the new 45 B.C., if you know what I mean.

Last year (45 B.C.) was like so crazy for me with just too much attention and crazed peasants trying to get a piece of me every single minute of every single day! Oh my God, can you believe that I just grew tired of it all!? I mean, puh-leeze—I am just a person like the rest of you, and just because I am extremely wealthy and attractive and happen to be unofficially dating <u>Julius Caesar</u> doesn't mean I don't put on my personally designed gowns the same way you do!! With servants! Hah! Don't we all!?

So, whatever, I know you feel me. Last year was crazy and now this year is more of the same with the people and the wanting and the touching and the me me me me me!! It's enough to just make you want to scream! And I have! Many times!

That's why I'm taking Caesarion my son with me to visit his dad in Rome next month (March) to visit the A-list Roman you all know from his power and his wealth and his good looks—J. Caesar. J.C. has promised he's going to do it up for me, with lavish dinners and even top-of-the-line transportation coming to pick me up for the trip from Egypt. All I have to say is he'd better live up to his promises—we are traveling in STYLE.

I want a four-horse chariot or I am NOT GOING ANYWHERE. And when I get into that four-horse chariot there better be a kick-ass Roman Gift Bag in there or J.C. ain't getting anything from me if you know what I mean. I am a walking billboard of publicity for that guy and that Roman empire and if he wants the people to continue to be obsessed with this "forbidden romance" between the two of us then he'd better give the girl what she deserves. Jewels. I want more jewels.

J.C. has also promised to help me get my new perfume (called ASP!) off the ground. It's dangerous-sounding, like the poisonous snake! Get it? Dangerous, like me. So, ladies—if you wanna be like Cleo here, all attractive and pretty and wealthy and sexy and dangerous, then ASP is what you want the men to smell. I think it'll be a big hit, and J.C. is gonna help me work some tie-ins with some of the big events in Rome this year to help up the awareness.

I've got more <u>photos</u> of me up in the gallery section, now—so go check me out. There's also a new page I've put up called "Cleo's Beauty Tips" which you can read <u>here</u> after ponying up some of those sesterces in your pocket. Pay up—and learn what you can do to have that man of your dreams that's just outside of your reach!

On an unrelated note, signed drawings of me are all sold out—when we get our next shipment of granite and slate we'll have the artist create some more and we'll make them available again for purchase! I'll be blogging from Rome in March, so see you then!

From: **http://www.john_d_rockefeller.com/blog/**

Subject: **Today's Blog from Mr. Rockefeller**

As Mr. Rockefeller is unable to blog for himself today, I will be blogging in his place per his request. This is his personal blogger Nancy, as you very well know by now, as I have blogged for Mr. Rockefeller for the last 112 days. You can read my entries, as written for Mr. Rockefeller, in the <u>Standard Oil Archives</u>.

In yesterday's post, which I wrote for Mr. Rockefeller, I answered a variety of e-mails from those who wished to communicate a wide array of business opportunities or ideas to Mr. Rockefeller. As I mentioned yesterday, Mr. Rockefeller appreciates your ideas but is simply way too busy to respond to them. I will say Bill J's idea for a car powered by something other than gas so that the United States is not dependent on oil was intriguing, but obviously the kind of scenario that is better suited to a science fiction novel. Mr. Rockefeller, to whom I brought up the previously suggested idea, did not respond except for flashing me a smug look which, after 112 days blogging for him, has come to mean, "What are you, stupid?"

Today, Mr. Rockefeller would like me to blog for him about his childhood and his memories and experiences that brought him to where he is today.

Mr. Rockefeller was born in Richford, New York, and was one of six children. As he grew, Mr. Rockefeller was a stellar student, a religiously anchored young man, and an extremely driven individual. Mr. Rockefeller eventually would leave high school to enroll in business classes, which would be the beginning of his huge oil empire.

Mr. Rockefeller would also like you to know this quick fact: Did you know that Mr. Rockefeller's first job was as a bookkeeper where he only made $25 a month? It's quite amazing to see how far this business tycoon has come!

Mr. Rockefeller would like everyone to know that even as a child he had lofty goals for himself and he just kept dreaming and going after his goals. Mr. Rockefeller would also like you to know that he believes if you don't give up on your goals you will eventually reach that which you desire. He also wants you to know that he is not a fan of apples, so if you're thinking about sending a gift basket of apples, to refrain from doing that, since they will just end up in the garbage.

Mr. Rockefeller wanted me to make sure you knew his current <u>e-mail address</u> in the event you would like to send him an idea, a comment or a question about all of his writings here on his personal blog. He appreciates your thoughts on the columns he writes, and is always open to requests for subject matter although you must be aware that since it does take time to write the blog entries, Mr. Rockefeller can't promise that he'll choose your subject to write about! He thanks you for reading daily and can't wait for you to read his blog tomorrow!

From: http://www.vince_lombardi.com/blog/

Subject: Is Playing Football a Fantasy?

Some people suck at winning.

In fact, most people are losers. That's why people revel in the success of winners. If everyone was a winner, or most people were winners, then winners wouldn't much matter in the world since everyone would have the ability to win. But they don't. In fact, most of you reading this probably lose more than you care to admit.

No, winning is a rarity, set aside for those who are disciplined and dedicated and have the ability to work themselves to within an inch of their life. Winning is a treasure for those willing to search long and hard. Winning is reserved for a very small percentage of society's men—for just one percent of the entire hundred.

That is, until now.

As a coach, I know what it's like to win. I've finished second only twice in my life. And after those moments, I vowed to never finish second again. (And I didn't.) People often ask me what it's like to feel the rush of taking a team to the top. They often say that they wish they could experience the same thing, but they're stuck being accountants or bankers or lawyers. Thing is, running a football team is no different than running any other kind of organization. Principles are the same. The object is to beat the other guy and to win. It got me to thinking—how could America's losers at least get an opportunity to feel that same rush?

That's when I came up with the idea for Lombardi's Football Fantasy Club.

Launching today (just click on the above link)—you'll be able to be the coach of a football team just like me! From a selection of today's NFL athletes you'll pick your players, then follow them through an entire season of game play. Every time one of your players does something great, something truly heroic and amazing—you'll get the credit you deserve for picking him and coaching him. You'll be considered a winner! Just like me!

But just like the real world—in this Fantasy Club, losers aren't worth crap. If you lose a game or the majority of the players you've picked are making bad plays and consistently making mistakes, you will be ridiculed and eventually kicked out of the Fantasy Club. Because losers don't ever get ahead in the real world, and they won't here either.

And there won't be any of those losers-play-losers games like in the real-world NFL. There will be no second place bowl game. If you lose, you will be kicked out, your user name will be deleted, you'll lose all the money you put into the game and the Lombardi Football Fantasy Club will deny that you ever existed. Losers need not ever come back! Losers often face this kind of disappointment in life, and the Lombardi Football Fantasy Club will be no different. If you lose, you will feel like you have just ruined your entire life—and you will have! Real stakes. Real situations. Real life.

Are you a winner or a loser? Will you triumph or will you fail? Will you show your greatness or show your loser qualities to the entire world? It's a question that you can answer—just by joining.

Thanks to all my great readers, by the way! You guys are all champions in my mind and together each and every one of you has made my website a smashing success!! Pat yourselves on the back, people! You are so great!

Questions or concerns? E-mail Vince.

From: **http://www.es.ferdinand_magellan.com/blog/**
Subject: **Explo-rants!**

Look, it's no surprise I wanna be an explorer. You've heard it a thousand times. I know I can be one. I've studied. I'm in a pretty good place to do it. In fact, in a few weeks I'm gonna head to sea for the first time with Francisco de Almeida on our way to India—but that's not what I wanna talk about.

There are explorers . . . A-List explorers. And they are ranting and raving about the most ludicrous, insignificant things on their blogs without ever stopping to realize that they're ALREADY FAMOUS EXPLORERS! How many people would die to be an explorer!? How many kids want to grow up to be just like them!? Yet what do they do? They forget where they came from and just rant and rave (I call it "explo-rants") instead of being humble like they should.

Why not check out Vasco da Gama's Weblog? Mr. "Admiral of the Indian Ocean" who was the first to sail from Europe to India doesn't fill up his pages enlightening the youth of today with just how it became possible or advice on how to reach such heights. His post from last week, Extreme Ultimate Admiral, spends five pages arguing that being called "Admiral" is not nearly enough for the amazing feats he and his crew have accomplished. What an ego this guy's got! Totally turned me off.

What about Hernán Cortés's Blog? Have you been to this monstrosity of ego-ness? Yes, sure, he conquered Mexico for Spain but for that does he really deserve acres of land and Indian slaves? Cortés blogs about wanting more slaves because he's really busy but I think this is just another example of the fame and fortune going to an explorer's head! I mean, what does he need all those Indian slaves for? Sure, give him a couple, but why not give some of those Indian slaves to the needy people? The people who don't have ANY Indian slaves? Man, when I read that about Cortés, well, I'm not gonna go out and buy any more of his famous maps anymore. I'd rather give my money to an explorer who deserves it!

And don't even get me started on Sebastian Cabot. This guy, you probably don't even know who he is! Yeah, yeah—so his dad is John Cabot, who discovered Nova Scotia (i.e., Canada). Big deal! Right? So his dad is famous. Well because of that, Sebastian thinks he should be famous too. In fact, while Sebastian rants about how he deserves his own ships for exploring this new-found land he forgets to tell you that he was the one who was involved in that "discovering China" fiasco. All that press and, in the end, it wasn't China at all. Sheesh. The kids of famous explorers make me sick.

Finally, it pains me to even say it, but <u>Christopher Columbus</u> is losing his marbles. All the guy talks about on his blog now is the fact that he <u>hates the names of his ships</u> and he rants about it constantly. Chris, you discovered America. Talk about that. Stop talking about stuff that doesn't matter years after the glory days are over.

All I have to say to all of you is this: when I become famous . . . when I finally accomplish something like, oh I don't know, circumnavigating the globe or something, don't expect me to whine all day long about the weight of all the gold on my back or my servants or my title. If I'm an explorer, and I get to do what I have always dreamed of . . . then I'm not going to take it for granted. I'm going to enjoy it and respect it and give advice to others who were once in my position.

Man, these prima donna explorers and their inflated egos have just about made me lose my lunch.

What about you? Do you agree? <u>Let me know</u>.

From: **http://www.spartacus.com/blog/**
Subject: **Gladiator School, Week 34**

Ugh, I am so over this whole gladiator school thing.

Last week we learned how to fight blindfolded and while on horseback. The week before that, I got a chunk bitten out of my left leg by a wild boar. The week before that, while fighting on horseback with a gladius and while wearing a visored helmet (that you can hardly even see through), I got a spear in my right foot from that idiotic Gillias. The week before that, full armor. The week before that, using the noose. Tridents, daggers, nets, wearing nothing, wearing a shield, a visor, or even a full tunic in the hot sun. There are lions and wild dogs and a variety of other wild animals you would never want to spend long periods of time with. Yet here I am, against my will, doing just that.

Sigh. Being a slave sure had its advantages.

Sometimes at night, whichever of us are still alive sit around and talk about our fond memories about being slaves for Roman families. The whippings and the fetching and the never-ending fatigue. It was heaven compared to this.

Tomorrow, we fight in Ordinarii (or pairs)—one gladiator against another. Tonight there were at least some laughs to be had, each of us practicing raising our finger—when you beat another gladiator you're supposed to raise a finger to the audience so they can decide if the loser should live or die! That was sorta fun, each of us raising our finger to one another and letting the others decide LIVE or DIE! People were chanting DIE more often than LIVE, but we discussed it for some time and we think that mostly, if one of us had lost a gladiator match that the audience would probably say LIVE instead of DIE. No one wants to see that much blood. People hate the sight of it. Of that I'm sure. So, at least there's a silver lining to this whole thing.

Oh! Some good news, actually. Looks like Lentulus Batiatus, who owns the school here in Capua, has decided to give the current survivors their own personal contact mailboxes. So, if you want to correspond with me while I'm incarcerated here, feel free to send a message to <u>Spartacus@mountvesuviusacademy.net</u>. I'll try to respond as quickly as I can, but know that sometimes I am simply out of commission.

Think good thoughts for me and the others. Hopefully things here at the Gladiator School will get better next week. Probably not, but I can hope, right?

Oh, and if you're interested (my old slavemasters were) you can see my <u>report card</u>. I'm doing pretty good so far, no matter that I find all of this a little bit forced upon me. I did extremely well in "stabbing and slicing while blindfolded," which is, I guess, pretty neat.

From: **http://www.janeausten.uk/weblog/**

Subject: **He Who Shall Remain Unnamed Due to Embarrassing Results**

"He" Who Shall Remain Unnamed came quietly into my life a mere two weeks prior accompanied by a selection of digital correspondences that were both witty and respectful.

Previously, I had mentioned my <u>astonishment</u> at how well-read and intelligent he seemed. He was eloquent, considerate and extremely encouraging. I quickly felt as if I knew his character. 'Twas over the course of many exchanges that I felt as if "He" Who Shall Remain Unnamed was not a rogue but a true gentleman in the finest sense of the word. But perhaps such familiarity was due to the fact that "He" was not a stranger after all, but instead was closer to my heart than any of us could have imagined.

Perhaps he was Mr. Collinsworth, the barrister with whom I'd shared a cup of tea months earlier. You may recall how, after asking him the reason for his great success in all but love, the colour left his face most promptly. Or perhaps Ernest Doyle, the local businessman with whom I once shared a carriage into town? Upon my suggesting that his hand was in the most inopportune of places (my knee), he stammered an apology and disappeared soon after. Perhaps it was a man with whom I had interacted, but whose confidence for one reason or another needed a costume from which to approach me.

My solitary lifestyle has indeed grown tiresome, which I can embarrassingly illustrate through the short writings I have submitted to such places as <u>RespectableLadies.com</u> and <u>BritainsBest.net</u>. There, I have found myself, not the subject of a chorus of enthusiasm, but instead a silence most deafening.

Perhaps that is why I hoped for the best with "He" Who Shall Remain Unnamed due to embarrassing results. The results of which, I will now explain to you.

Consequences being what they were, it had been previously agreed upon that the two of us (having successfully justified a social meeting through our quick and charismatic textual banter) would meet for afternoon tea at a local establishment. "He" insisted that it was unnecessary to forward me a picture, as the surprise would be far more satisfying. At the time, such a suggestion seemed playful, like that of a romantic rogue—and so in spite of my desire to see "him" ahead of time, I agreed.

The preparation took hours—I studied his words, making note of subjects he spoke enthusiastically about. I recalled stories that I might speak of, showing "him" that the similarities between the two of us were more than coincidental. I dressed in attire that was not casual yet not elegant. A measured presentation of sorts, as such, to not overexcite or underwhelm. With the hour arriving quickly, I made my way out the house and down to the establishment.

There I stood, at the time in question, awaiting my intellectual equal . . . My mysterious correspondent with whom I'd shared hundreds of stories and personal information. Yet, looking around there was no one there except for a boy about the age of twelve. Perhaps younger. He was sucking on candy, which gave away his age almost immediately.

Yet he suddenly stood to approach me, his hand outstretched.

"Ms. Austen?" he spoke, hiding his candy behind his back. *"Fancy that tea now?"*

*   *   *

I have disabled my digital mailbox until further notice, as I do not believe any good can come from the correspondences between faceless individuals and myself. If there is love to be had here, in this strange new landscape—I do not believe it is for me.

And besides, I have a book to complete.

From: **http://www.confucius.ch/blog/**

Subject: • • •

The honest man knows not when he is being honest—an effort must never be made to discern between honesty and dishonesty, as the honest man is honest all the time. And then, how can an honest man who is honest all the time know anything different from such honesty? To him, there is no need to consider a lie. If his soul does not lie, all that comes forth from his lips is the truth.

So too is the case for the subject line of this digital page of words.

When does a subject fully encompass the subject that follows? When do words prepare us for other words to follow? A word can never hold the meaning of other words. A phrase can never enlighten us to future phrases. The wise man will never read a subject line and be satisfied. He must dig deeper for a passage's full understanding.

The blogged man, he who rises with the sun and gazes upon thousands upon thousands of words as crafted by his fellow man—he does not need a subject line to direct his path. Yet those who do not familiarize themselves with such prose, who are unfamiliar with such style and shape—they put all their worth into such limited prose.

The righteous man gazes upon a subject line and gives it no weight. Yet the inferior man, saddled with weight already due to his lack of direction, gazes upon such words with faith and dedication. To the inferior man, the subject line says all. To the righteous man, the subject line says nothing.

The inferior man speaks at the completion of reading the subject line and summarizes what he is about to read, while the righteous man reads the subject line and imagines what he is about to digest.

That is why the righteous man has no need for a subject line on his blog. That is why I have no need for a subject line on this blog. A man with no subject line on his blog (or his correspondences, in fact) has a life full of possibilities, while the man who is desperate to put prose where it defines other prose, has a life already decided for him.

(Tomorrow, I, Confucius, will address the righteous man's lack of necessity for a digital counter, and the inferior man's necessity for vertigo-inducing background images.)

From: **http://www.william_wrigley_jr.com/blog/**

Subject: **Father's Business**

So far, Chicago has treated the Wrigley family well. Father's soap business continues to succeed—Wrigley's scouring soap is a favorite among the merchants and customers and Father has asked me to help think up the next step in ensuring growth for the company. Perhaps adding baking soda to the overall product line might be a good idea—these are ideas I am still debating.

Nevertheless, Father invited a selection of business contacts over to the house the other evening for an elaborate dinner—I suggested to him this was a good idea because it would make Wrigley's top merchants feel a part of the family, and thus, they would be much more willing to get the word out about the products. And indeed, it appeared as if it was a good idea, that is, until dinner was served.

There, as the lot of us were attempting to talk about a variety of business issues, a strange, startling sound was coming from the other end of the table. That sound, of course, was coming from the mouth of a local businessman (whose name I will keep to myself). As he tore through his dinner, he repeatedly chewed voraciously—smacking his lips and allowing others at the table to see inside his mouth as he repeatedly chomped down upon his dinner. It was, honestly, the most disgusting sight I have ever seen.

Even worse was this individual's lack of respect—the way in which he would continue to speak and insert himself into the conversation while continuing to chew. Honestly, and I'm not quite sure why I've never noticed this before, but the act of chewing and speaking with one's mouth wide open communicates a lack of respect to the others at the table—chew and speak at the same time and you might as well be saying, *"I don't care what you have to say, it's what I have to say that's most important here!"*

No one said anything, mind you, which made the situation even more grating on our nerves, as this individual continued to do so through the entire meal and well through the dessert portion of the evening. Just picture it—someone yammering away with their jaw clenching and unclenching, mouth open for all to see, saliva being mixed throughout. Even with his mouth closed, seeing a man repeatedly chew as if he was attempting to work his food to his will is abhorrent.

When the evening ended, I expressed these thoughts to Father, who agreed wholeheartedly. It seems he too found the whole situation to have ruined the mood of the dinner.

Tomorrow I will return to brainstorming for what Wrigley's next product shall be. I have some good ideas that I'd prefer to keep to myself for the moment—but will, as always, let you know as soon as the family is in agreement.

From: **http://www.attila_the_hun.com/blog/**
Subject: **Attila, On the Road!**

So, yeah—I'm on the road. Doing my whole tour thing with my whole entourage supporting me while I do it. Kick-ass guys, really. They've totally got my back, ya know? They make this whole "on the road" thing totally doable.

Well, we've been all over the place but we picked up and headed over to start our tour in Italy this last week 'cause it had been planned for a while now. And once something's planned, you gotta keep that shit in line.

Okay. Let me just say . . . I totally killed this week at Aquileia.

By the time I was done with my whole routine in that city, literally no one was left standing—I had totally slayed them and the entire town! Totally kicked ass! The kind of success you can't always count on, but the people of Aquileia, at least those who are even able to speak after my appearance there, well—they'd agree. I totally killed.

Here's some <u>pictures</u> of me and the guys standing near a crowd, all dyin' for us.

Don't get me wrong, though—even before we did our thing at Aquileia, we razed the roof throughout most of Italy. I mean, at every single town, with every single group of townspeople—we did things up like crazy. Never a dry eye. Totally bowing down to me after I did my thang. Totally rocked their world.

The groupies, you gotta believe, are coming out of the woodwork. What do you expect?! They hear about the tour, how I'm totally kicking ass, and they wanna hang with Attila and his boyz. I got women sending me rings, wanting to hook up, and BS like that. But no one stands a chance next to my latest conquest—this hottie named Ildico. I mean, she's the kind of girl that'll give you a nosebleed and cause you to choke to death she's so hot. I'm thinkin' that when we get back to the palace—another marriage may have to happen.

Until then, you can keep checkin' in here to see where we're at—in case you wanna come down and join the party. Don't forget—we got that <u>mailing list</u> that you can sign up for—we'll let you know the next location we're heading off to so you get a good head start on us!

<u>E-mail</u> with questions.

From: **http://www.johannes_gutenberg.de/gutenblog/**

Already have an account? Sign in:
Username: Password: **(?)**

SIGN IN ☐ Remember me **(?)**

what's a gutenblog? TAKE A TOUR

Publish thoughts
Get feedback
Post photos
Go mobile

3 easy steps:

1. Create a gutenblog
2. Name your gutenblog
3. Choose a print+style

Forget about the printing press, your gutenblog allows you to share thoughts digitally, without ink!

CREATE YOUR GUTENBLOG →

RECENT NEWS

King Henry VI of England uses his gutenblog in a war of words with Richard, Duke of York.

The Official Frankfurt Book Fair blog talks about outdated printing presses.

The Pope Nicholas V gutenblog prints letters from mourners, worldwide.

Lazar Brankovic's political gutenblog goes live, in his quest to become king of Serbia.

From: **http://www.lewis_carroll.com/blog/**

Subject: **Vanished**

Oscar, the oft-egotistical feline who would (I believe) much prefer a meal than my company, has vanished.

Here is a <u>picture</u>.

My poetry, seemingly suffering from the lack of moral support as provided by my partner in crime, has come to a standstill as I attempt to locate the mischievous little troublemaker. This is not, as I have <u>written before</u>, a surprising development. Often, Oscar has sat on the love seat beside my desk while I am attempting to squeeze blood from a stone. One second I can turn to him for advice, and the next moment he has completely disappeared into thin air.

I often get up, spin around, and there he is yet again—smiling the widest grin imaginable without smiling whatsoever. I suspect it's the whiskers, and the way in which they vibrate—much like the energy inside of all children. Oscar, it seems, has a little child inside of him as well.

You may recall the riddles I posted <u>last month</u> which were sparked to my mind through an almost one-sided conversation with the little creature. My queries, the likes of which could never be answered by a normal everyday house cat, were answered in kind by the little creature—with facial expressions and nose twitches. To every question I posed, Oscar had another question to ask me. Never an answer. That is for sure.

Yet tonight, the cat has gone completely missing. I checked outside and down the street past the pub but he is nowhere in the vicinity. For a moment, while perched out the front door at the street's level, I could have sworn he appeared to me, yet the image was gone before I could comprehend it. The mind playing tricks, it seems—all when it comes to my little furry friend.

I suspect he's somewhere within a mile or two of the house, so I ask those reading to peruse the picture and keep an eye out for the smiling critter. If you find him, approach him cautiously and don't ask him a thing. Just grab him and send a message to lewiscarroll@webtech.uk.

I'm heading out now to look. More later.

Update: As soon as I posted this message above, he appeared behind the couch. Strange, since I looked there before. Nonetheless—he's safe and sound. Thank you!

From: **http://www.jack_kerouac.com/moblog/**

Subject: **On the Road, Sort of . . .**

I'm on a road . . . but not the kind of road with strangers blindly speeding by towns and cities so fast that it's all a blur, the kind of blur that life is when you don't stop and open your eyes long enough to see what's right in front of your face, which often isn't much at all but it's the discovery of realizing there's nothing out there in front of your face that frees you from the lack of knowledge you had before you stopped to take a look . . .

Neal Cassady and I hung last night and we emptied quite a few bottles and he started telling me that he's leaving town, going on his own Odyssey of sorts, and just like any journey like that can't be undertaken by just one man he wanted to know if me, yours truly, would join him on the adventure of a lifetime, and not to say this adventure would simply be the only adventure under such a heading but in fact the beginning of many adventures across this poverty-stricken, ego-controlled, powerless society of people all trying to break out of the bonds keeping them quiet and conservative and tired and clueless.

Sigh. Tired. Fatigue. When Neal said such things to me I'd been ending three weeks straight sitting in front of the glowing screen over in the corner of my apartment, undertaking my own adventure of a lifetime in the digital sense—scouring the words and the images and the people who make up the entire landscape of the digital underworld which all comes streaming through a small wire and into my world and into the device which lights up the room and lights up my thoughts, for all I can think about is that I am here, alone, sitting at this monitor and gazing into it and their lives, and at the same time they are doing the same thing. But three weeks is not an entire lifetime, and how can one abandon such a quest to see everything there is to see after only three weeks of a journey? I had more to do, more to say and more to write, all through this digital journal and thereby interacting with the rest of the individuals communicating through their own one-way mirror. Hitchhiking across the country would take years compared to simply turning on the glowing technological marvel in the corner!

Neal asked me again, this time more seriously, if I would accompany him "on the road" where we could experience the people and the sights and the sounds of the entire country. But as I told him, why go outside when you can sit right here in one place and see and hear the entire country without ever leaving the safety of one's pad? There's no reason to leave, no reason to venture out into the cold, dark world when sitting here provides all the same experiences, to which Neal asked "well, what about touching, the tactile feelings of real people" to which I responded "it's completely bullshit" because I've touched more people than I care to remember, and now sitting here with this glowing screen before me, I have everything I could have ever wanted, and can have it all in less time than it takes to down a swig from this bottle I'm holding between my legs as I type this out to you right now.

Neal left this morning for his journey. I'll try to keep track of him on the road from here.

I hope he got an e-mail address before he left.

From: **http://www.niccolo_machiavelli.fr/blog/**

Subject: **To All My Closest Friends!**

YOU. Yes, YOU. Bubby.

Glad you came back to visit! Can I just say that I've been
totally thinking about you lately and wondering when you'd be
coming back!? You're not just a number here on my stats page—you
are one of the few who I care to see visit my blog. Someone I
feel like I can talk to. You know? How do I know who you are?
Only my closest allies know of this URL and so if you are reading this, we are totally thick as thieves. And thank God,
because I have some things to get off my chest. To just my closest friends.

Let's talk about the Medici. You know, Lorenzo de' Medici—back in
power now in Florence after so much time has passed. Yours
truly, and I don't know if I mentioned this <u>before</u>, is no longer
in a position to exercise my sharp political suggestions and
insights. And you know what!? That's a good thing for YOU and
for ME, bubby.

Here's what's up—I'm starting the <u>Machiavelli Network</u>! Haha,
yeah, right!?

Exciting, I know. You're just desperate to know what it is,
right!? Well, let me tell you before I ramble on much further.
The Machiavelli Network is a closed, exclusive, online community
for those who are my FRIENDS. So far, the Machiavelli Network
has over 300 members, including some who are at the highest
positions in the current government. (I must keep their names a
secret, but I swear to the Lord this is true!)

The more people we can get to join the network, the more sites
who abandon their current <u>Medici.com</u> network and move over to

the Machiavelli Network will find that it is a decision that is well worth making. We're looking for people in influential positions in Italy—people who have power and respect who would be willing to express the opinions of the Machiavelli Network to those around them. No, we don't want to pressure people to think like us—we just want everyone to be aware of the alternative point of view! Sure, if they agree with us, wonderful. But our goal isn't to strong-arm anyone (like the other guys do). So . . . where do you come in, you ask? Simple.

In order to join the Machiavelli Network simply send me the application fee (yes it's sizable, but you're going to get it back tenfold) and you'll be immediately added to the exclusive network. Then, it's up to you to get ten more people to join! Easy, I know! And here's the best part . . .

Each of those ten people . . . they pay you the same fee that you paid me. Already you've made ten times your money and added to the value of the Machiavelli Network! And each time one of those ten people gets another person to join, you get 25% of the fee they have to pay. You can do this from sitting at home on the farm—you can stop working period. Because after you get ten people to join, your only job will be to go and pick up the money that people are offering you.

If we work together, we can make this the most powerful, politically influential network ever. I'm committed to it and to YOU, my very good friends.

If you have any questions, feel free to submit a support ticket.

By the way, I'm also working on a book. More on that later. But for now, thanks so much for stopping by, YOU. Love ya, bubby!

From: **http://www.vlad_the_impaler.com/dracula-blog/**
Subject: **Weekend Impaling in Transylvania**

'Twas a busy weekend for the one and only Vlad III Dracul, Prince of Wallachia.

It seems as though the killing of thousands of Turks, which yours truly Vlad III Dracul, Prince of Wallachia, oversaw over the last few weeks, made me generously feel for the people of Wallachia. For they had been denied the presence of me, Vlad III Dracul, for weeks on end, and as such it made them sad. So I returned, Prince of Wallachia, bringing smiles to their faces . . .

Yet not every one of my loyal subjects was smiling, even though Vlad III Dracul was in their presence. There were some, poverty-stricken and ill, whose lives seemed in total disrepair. And so, the generous Vlad III Dracul, Prince of Wallachia, gathered them together for a wonderful meal in my great hall. The unproductive, the ill, the hungry, the handicapped were all welcome! And I was there, too—Vlad III Dracul, Prince of Wallachia! The great wise leader of Wallachia! They ate and drank without a care!

I asked them if they wished to never have to worry about anything ever again—to be without a care in the world. Their response, of course, was that of enthusiasm. I promised I could give them such relief.

Then I had my men lock up the hall and light it on fire. Hehehehehehe! Let no man say that Vlad III Dracul, Prince of Wallachia, is a leader without humor!

More of the same on Saturday—lots of impaling to get through. Gosh, I suspect we impaled at least forty-three people around town. As I type this, I'm looking down and out of Poenari Castle—at the edge of the city there stand hundreds of people impaled on huge wooden staffs. And, I have to be honest as I look at the sight before me . . .

It's just not symmetrical. Doesn't seem even to me.

I have told my men a THOUSAND TIMES, that if they cannot arrange these impaled individuals in some sort of shape that is pleasing to look at, I . . . Vlad III Dracul, Prince of Wallachia, will be the laughingstock of Romania! A square, a circle, some kind of triangle. A dodecahedron. Whatever. But when I spy a few impaled people on sticks way off to the side of nowhere near the others, it makes my blood boil. I may just have to impale the impalers if they don't show pride in their work. I'll hire new impalers to impale the current impalers who can't impale to save their lives!

That's the problem—you hire these people to impale other people and before long they're not looking where they shove the sharpened staff . . . Sometimes the bodies fall off the staff because of the shoddy workmanship of the impalers . . . I don't know—I think Vlad III Dracul needs to remotivate these men to do a better job.

Sunday, I signed up for a <u>Gutenblog</u>. No ink required, they say. I suspect I will be using this on a daily basis to inform you of my wonderful ideas, intelligent thoughts and future plans for our cities and towns.

From: **http://www.malcolmX.edu/blog/**

Subject: **What Brought You Here and Why You Should Now Leave**

It is quite obvious to me that my brothers and sisters who are involved in our cause to take back our freedom have no trouble finding their way to this blog.

Unfortunately, there are many who find their way here by accident, who should never be here in the first place, and who I urge to remove themselves as quickly as they arrive—their visits are a result of these recent searches:

• Malcolm XXX

• Xtra Tuna, Please

• Why does X mark the spot?

• X-Rated Panthers

• Freedom from X-Rays

• Big X, Little X

• Is Lamb good for you?

• X-men comic #1

• Who is Racer X?

• How to treat mosque bites?

If you have found your way here through any of the above search strings or any others that do not involve <u>Malcolm X</u>, <u>Muslim Mosque, Inc.</u> or <u>The Organization of Afro-American Unity</u> you **are in the wrong place**.

From: **http://www.john_wayne.com/blog/**
Subject: **What's in a Name?**

Marion isn't a girl's name.

You may or may not know that Marion is the name I was born with. Marion became "Duke," which became "John Wayne." But Marion is still the name on my birth certificate and on a bunch of my official documents, and personally I don't think that the name "Marion" sounds female at all.

Now, if you're talkin' about Marian with an "an," that is definitely a girly-sounding name. Or Marione with an "one" at the end—yes, I can see where a person with that should probably be wearing an apron and cooking dinner for her husband. And even Maryione or MaryAnne or Marionne. Girly, girly, girly.

But Marion is totally a macho guy's name. It is. I mean, look at it. I've written it out hundreds and hundreds of times on a piece of paper, just to practice it . . . you know? And it looks like a man's man kind of name. It's the kind of name that fits a cowboy or a soldier or a hero. You know? *"Oh my gosh, that man just killed a hundred Nazis and saved my life!"* *"What was his name!? All I know is his first name—Marion!"* *"Yes. It IS a very masculine name!"*

I think you catch my drift.

So, a lot of <u>people</u> have been writing in asking why I changed from one pretty macho heroic name to John Wayne. Did you ever stop to think that Marion and Wayne are sort of the same? The change isn't that different. If you just pronounce the "on" at the end of Marion, and the "ne" at the end of Wayne—yes, I think you'll hear it! The same sound to the names. However, the name "John Wayne" is better for Hollywood, but not because the name Marion is girly or that I don't like the name. I love the name. It totally fits who I am. Sometimes, I even use the name myself when I'm just sitting around somewhere just to show them that I'm not embarrassed by the name.

"Marion would like a beer, please." And then they give Marion a beer.

Besides, why would I even write all of this about my really great first name if I was embarrassed by it? It's a great name, really it is. Seriously. It totally is.

My parents were smart. That's the plain honest-to-God truth. They picked a good one for a guy like me, and that's why I'll never change my birth certificate or any official documents when it comes to my name. (Besides, I've checked—you can't change that stuff anyway, so it's not worth worrying about.)

Now, just 'cause I'm okay with the name doesn't mean you can start calling me that. It'll just get confusing, so we'll stick with John Wayne or Duke or The Duke or The Biggest Star in American Cinema. Just not Marion.

Okay? Okay.

From: **http://www.copernicus.de/blog/**

Subject: READ THIS!! LOOK NOW! **EARTH NOT CENTER OF UNIVERSE!!**

IF YOU READ THE ABOVE SUBJECT LINE YOU NOW KNOW THAT THIS INFORMATION I HAVE RECENTLY BECOME AWARE OF IS OF EXTREME IMPORTANCE TO ALL IN THE ENTIRE WORLD!!!! THIS INFORMATION MUST BE PASSED FROM ONE TO ANOTHER UNTIL EVERYONE IS IN POSSESSION OF THE INFORMATION!! OTHERWISE, I FEAR THAT SUCH INFORMATION MAY NEVER FIND ITS WAY TO THE PUBLIC.

CONTRARY TO WHAT YOU'RE BEING TOLD. CONTRARY TO WHAT YOU'VE BEEN LED TO BELIEVE. CONTRARY TO EVERYTHING YOU'VE READ ABOUT THE HEAVENS—THE EARTH IS **NOT NOT NOT NOT NOT NOT NOT** THE CENTER OF THE UNIVERSE. IT IS **NOT NOT NOT** WHAT THEY'VE TOLD YOU. EVERYTHING YOU BELIEVE IS WRONG.

I HAVE RESEARCH THAT PROVES THAT EVERYTHING **REVOLVES AROUND THE SUN** AND I CALL THIS MY "HELIOCENTRIC" PHILOSOPHY ABOUT THE HEAVENS.

HAVE YOU READ THE WORDS OF <u>CICERO</u> OR <u>PLATO</u>? HAVE YOU STUDIED WHAT THE ANCIENTS BELIEVED ABOUT THE MOVEMENT OF THE EARTH? HAVE YOU THROWN AWAY YOUR FALSE BELIEFS AND ARE YOU NOW OPEN TO BELIEVING THE TRUTH? BECAUSE **THE TRUTH IS OUT THERE!**

<u>LINK</u> TO AN ARTICLE ON GEOCENTRIC THEORY—TOTALLY WRONG!!!

<u>LINK</u> TO GEORGE RHETICUS'S BLOG, MY DEAR FRIEND WHO HAS CONVINCED ME THAT THE TRUTH OF THE UNIVERSE AND HOW IT MOVES MUST BE PUBLISHED HERE FOR ALL THE WORLD TO SEE.

<u>LINK</u> TO "COMMENTARIOLUS"—MY ELABORATED THOUGHTS ON THIS THEORY, THE EVIDENCE AS TO WHY THIS IS TRUE, AND WHY YOU SHOULD **NOT BELIEVE WHAT THE OTHERS ARE SAYING**.

LINK TO THIS PAGE AS OFTEN AS POSSIBLE. POINT PEOPLE IN THIS DIRECTION. WE ARE LIVING IN A WORLD THAT IS NOT WHAT IT SEEMS AND IT IS UP TO A SMALL GROUP OF US TO GET THE WORD OUT BEFORE WE ARE QUASHED BY THE "RESPECTED SCIENTISTS" OF THE WORLD. TIME IS RUNNING OUT!

<u>CONTACT ME</u> WITH QUESTIONS.

From: **http://www.michelangelo.it/blog/**

Subject: **Project Impasse**

The seventeen-foot-high block of marble was delivered yesterday. So, too, were additional chiseling tools necessary for the project. Today at dawn, I expected the project to commence.

And then my model, David, discovered he had a problem.

In fact, in all fairness, I should rephrase. David did not **have** a problem ... he **is** a problem. Suddenly, after months of discussion and him being well aware of what this project entailed, he has now decided he does NOT WANT TO POSE NUDE!!

He arrived today in clothing wrapped tightly around his torso. When I suggested it was time to begin, he stood up on the pedestal and refused to take off the clothes when I prompted him to do so.

"Take them off," I told him.

"I'm afraid I cannot," he said.

"What are you afraid of?" I asked him.

"I'm not pleased with how I look," he replied.

"You look perfect," I assured him. *"I will do your body justice in my sculpture."*

"You may think I look perfect," he said. *"But you don't wake up and go to sleep with this body every single day of your life. I can see the imperfections in it."*

"You are crazy," I told him. *"Now take off your clothes."*

"No," he said, crossing his arms.

"My patience is waning," I told him. *"You agreed. This project has been commissioned. Everything has been set in motion. I must begin today."*

"You don't like what I'm wearing?" he asked.

"It's not that I don't like what you're wearing," I said cautiously. *"But the statue I planned on creating requires the perfect male form, completely bare. That is why I chose you. You are perfect."*

"I don't believe you. You're just saying that to curry favor," he said.

"What do I need to say in order for you to believe me when I tell you that you have a beautiful body?" I asked.

"Look me in the eyes and really mean it," he said, nervously.

So I looked him in the eyes and told him again. He still was not willing to remove the garment and so I had to begin with his feet. HIS FEET.

I am hoping that after a night of thinking on this project, he will change his mind.

Hope, being the key word.

From: **http://www.j_edgar_hoover.com/confidentialBLOG/**

Subject: **New Pair of Shoes**

As always, this personal blog entry was passed through the offices of the FBI before it ended up here on my blog. This is, as I've explained before, ███████████████████████████████ if I want to express my personal thoughts in this capacity.

Now, on to the ██████ stuff!

This past weekend I went into █████ the city with my good friend ███████ and three ██████████ who he's been ██████████████████████ with lately. We had some drinks and dinner, and had a grand old time. ███████████████████████████ were very generous by providing us with a ████████████████ that was on the house, simply as ████████████████████████████ I may have given them.

More importantly, you will not guess what I found ██████████████████████████████? Next door to the restaurant, there in the display window was the most beautiful pair of ████████████ shoes I have ever seen in my life. ████████████████ heels, with a great ██████ over-the-top—███████████████████████████ friends agreed ████████████████████. After thinking about my finances for a little while, debating which ████████████ it might look good with, and if I really NEEDED a pair of shoes like that, I dropped the cash and picked up the pair ██████████████. I tried them on ████████████████████████████████, and we both agreed ███████████████ perfectly.

Later that night, after ████████████████████████ dinner at the ████████████████ Restaurant, we all went to ████████████████ where the six of us met up with ████████████ men ████████████████████. Well, since ████████████ place was just down the street we all ███████████████████████.

I'm still recouping from the entire night's ████████████████████, but let me just say that I had a ████████████████████ and was glad I got the opportunity to ████████████████, hang out with ██████████████████ and experience ████████████████.

Starting tomorrow, back to work—rooting out all the traitors and liars in this country. I will, as always, strive to do my best.

If you want to ███████ next weekend, get a hold of me at ████████████████.

From: **http://www.eva_peron.com/blog/**

Subject: **Buenos Aires!**

God, I am so relieved to be out of my boring, stinky little miserable town and here in Buenos Aires! This city is huge! It is more exciting than I ever imagined! Of course, things didn't turn out exactly how I'd hoped—remember when I told you about meeting Mr. X? The musician? And how he promised to make me a movie star here in Buenos Aires?

The guy disappeared like two weeks after getting here. What a you-know-what! Girls, do you hear what I'm saying!?

Well, things are good now. I just booked a few small radio jingle ads—singing and voice acting—and that's helped me get considered for this role in this small film! It also helps that, you know, I've met some producers lately . . . Wink, wink!! LOL! ROTFL!

Last night I was staying at B's place, who I met last week at an audition, and he was asking me what my dream was. You know, where I wanted to be in the end? It was so funny, I was all joking with him and saying how I wanted to be the ruler of Argentina!! You know, loved by all, respected by millions, that sorta thing. We laughed for hours. How about just being a movie star, he wondered. That sounded good to me!!

B says he thinks I'll make a great actress—he says he can tell from my presence. He says other people are saying it too. That makes me feel good, even excited about the future! Who knows! Maybe I'll be so huge in the movies that after I die they'll make a movie ABOUT me? LOL. What a joke.

Well if they do, I told B, they'd better make sure it's got a lot of music ('cause I love singing) and whoever plays me must be able to sing. You know, really be able to sing. How else could they act out the parts of my life going on right now without me singing for the radio and in movies and stuff!? You know? Someone good. Some really well regarded actress could play me. I mean, if I really become some huge actress like B says he thinks I will be—well, no B-listers.

Anyway, like THAT will ever happen. I have more luck becoming some kind of spiritual leader of Argentina before any of that ever happens.

LOL.

What a joke.

P.S.—I think I'm bored with B.

From: **http://www.hannibal.com/warblog/**

Subject: **Amazing Idea #45D**

War elephants.

I was sitting around last night with some of my other military commanders, drawing up plans for our march from Spain, over the Pyrenees and the Alps into northern Italy, when the idea hit me.

War elephants.

We affix them with saddles, sharpen their tusks, get them all bothered and angry, and take them into battle against the Romans. Horses, sure. We'll bring horses. But just think for a moment—if you're running into battle and you see me charging toward you on a war elephant what are you going to think?

You're going to think, uh oh, there's some guy running at me with a war elephant and that's way more dangerous than a war horse (even though we don't call them war horses) and you'll probably get out of the way as quickly as you possibly can because, well . . . war elephants.

It's a totally good idea, I think. War elephants. Say that a few times and don't tell me it doesn't send a shiver down your spine!

You can go ahead and chalk this one up with some of my other successful ideas, which include: <u>Amazing Idea #44A (Intimidating Capes)</u>, <u>Amazing Idea #43F (Incoherent Screams During Battle to Confuse)</u>, and the classic <u>Amazing Idea #12A (Dogs in Sheep's Clothing)</u>.

The more I think about it, the more I am confident that "war elephants" are not only visually scary but just hearing what we call them could cause some to back down against our forces before ever witnessing the battle at hand. I can imagine the conversation, can't you?

Roman #1: *"Did you hear, Hannibal's got war elephants."*

Roman #2: *"War elephants?"*

Roman #1: *"Yes, war elephants."*

Roman #2: *"Really? War elephants?"*

Roman #1: *"Yes. Seriously."*

Roman #2: *"Wow. War elephants."*

War elephants. I will let you know what the rest of my advisors think about the idea, but I'm open to any of your thoughts as well. Hannibal@hannibal.com.

From: **http://www.wild_bill_hickok.com/blog/**

Subject: **Spades, Clubs & Hearts**

My new wife, Agnes, keeps getting on my back about the poker playin'.

I love her with all my heart but she keeps sayin' it ain't a respectable thing to do, and that there are far better ways to be responsible. She keeps goin' on about how I'll never make a worthwhile living playin' poker and it's gonna be the death of me, she says. She throws a fit if she sees me playin' on the <u>Sitting Bull Online Poker Emporium</u>, which, by the way, is one of the few good things that's come out of this whole Native thing.

Playin' poker professionally is somethin' I'm very serious about—it ain't just some kind of game to pass the time with. It's serious business. If there's a game of poker goin' on in a town, that's my job. Better than workin' in some stage show (no offense to <u>Buffalo Bill's</u>) and better than bein' a marshal or even a gunfighter. Those are the dangerous professions, where in a split second you can end up with a bullet in your skull and have no money to show for it.

That's what I keep tellin' Agnes. Would she rather I be single-handedly trying to capture outlaws on the run? Would she rather I go back to bein' a constable? Holdin' people to the laws? A man is pretty much guaranteed a nice hot bullet in the craw for doin' a job like that where you make a lot of enemies. But not in poker. Like I always say, as long as you know when to hold 'em and know when to fold 'em and know when to walk away and know when to run and you never count your money while you're sittin' at the table—well, your safety is pretty much guaranteed.

Poker's a gentleman's game. Now that I'm in Deadwood, I wake my ass up and head on down to Nuttal & Mann's Saloon No. 10 where there's always a game goin' on. Not always an empty seat—but I'm so addicted to the game that no matter where there's an open slot, I'm sitting my butt down in it. Sometimes the room's so packed that the only seat left is the one with the back to the door . . . But you gotta do what you gotta do to get into a game, that's what I always say.

Besides, it's sorta an unspoken law that if a man's got cards in his hands, you never blindside a fella. It's a rule I live by, and I like to think everyone else does too.

Okay, I'll check back with y'all tomorrow! Headin' down to the saloon. I am feelin' lucky . . . Hooo boy. Luck luck luck luck luck.

From: **http://www.william_wallace.org/scot-blog/**

Subject: **Scotsmen! Meet up!**

Sons of Scotland—you have arrived here at the William Wallace blog, and by making that choice you have taken the first step in joining me and my other Scottish brothers in our crusade against the English!

The word has come to me from Andrew de Moray that the English army is approaching with over 10,000 strong. We must challenge their forces, no matter our lack of numbers. I ask that you come to fight now, as free men—since free men are what you are! But if we allow the English to take that away from us, then we will have nothing!!

Including <u>this really fun time-wasting online game</u>—check it out when you get a chance.

Yes, you may fight and you may die. Yes, if you run you may live . . . at least for a while. But years from now, when you're lying on your deathbed you will wish you had stood and fought for your freedom, on that one day, instead of living a life without it.

Will you join us?

I have arranged for a special <u>Battle of Stirling Bridge Meet-up</u>. Just click on the link to find out all the information. The location, the time we're to meet, and what we may need you to bring (i.e., weapons, supplies, food, etc.). As this will be a battle won by passion and not numbers, any and all Scots are welcome to meet up with us. In fact, they are urged to join this cause!

If you have friends who you think would also like to meet up with us at Stirling Bridge, feel free to copy the above link and send it to them. There is no charge or fee for participating—we are welcoming any and all to this event. Please be sure to submit your picture so we can know who's coming. We'd hate to identify you as one of the English and kill you, only to find out you were coming to meet up with us!

It's happened before, so . . . you know.

Join us, my brothers! JOIN US in our fight! Seriously, JOIN US. Every one of you who clicks on the link above and joins us will also receive the opportunity to possibly win something as well. Something extremely good.

Freedom!

From: **http://www.L_Frank_Baum.com/blog/**

Subject: **The Wicked Witch of the West Chicago**

Selling china door-to-door is not something I consider to be the best part of my day, although it does take up a great deal of my time and if I am someday able to write about such experiences (which is my ultimate wish) it may provide me with some interesting stories. Unfortunately, some days these stories are about my unfortunate experiences with mean-spirited and unhappy potential customers.

Today was one of those days.

I had gotten off to a late start already, so I was frustrated to begin with. I have been out this week in West Chicago pounding the pavement. It hasn't borne much fruit, as the neighborhood is populated by professionals—most everyone is off at work during the daylight hours. However, I did happen to find someone home at one house in particular.

The Witch, which I will call her from this point forward, had a sour look on her face when she noticed me standing there in my black suit and brand-new shoes—ready to negate anything I was about to say. But when I uncovered the place setting of china—her eyes lit up like someone desperate to have it. She welcomed me in, only after asking me to take off my shoes in the foyer, which I happily did. (It's not often you get invited in, so I thought this would perhaps be a sale.)

Once inside, the Witch perused the china, looking at herself in the reflection of the dinner plate. She did that for what seemed like minutes, obsessed with her own image. It was about that point that her children and their friends (about six little creatures running all in and around us at the kitchen table) came screaming at us . . . Honestly, they were everywhere. Under the table, on my knee, in the living room and dining room. In the midst of it all, one of these little monsters knocked a salad plate onto the floor, smashing it into a thousand pieces.

The Witch immediately flew off her handle, screaming wildly and chasing the little creatures around the room—eventually after she had chased them away, she took out her broom and got to cleaning up. She didn't even apologize, quickly revealing that she had no interest in these place settings, but wondered what brand my shoes were and if I would be willing to sell them to her.

My shoes? The Witch wanted my shoes. I told her that my shoes weren't for sale and quickly pulled my things together only to realize when I reached the front door that my shoes were gone. I asked her where they had gone and she pleaded innocence. I demanded that she give them back, to which she sweetly replied that she had no idea where they were. I threatened to stay right there until they were returned, which she ignored. She sat on the couch, eating an apple, pretending I wasn't even there.

I demanded again to get my shoes back. This Witch feigned innocence. She knew nothing about it and there was no more to be said. I eyed a half-full glass of water on the coffee table—thinking in this moment of frustration that I would throw it on her . . . but I refrained. My sanity meant more to me than this horrible creature and my pair of shoes, and so I walked out (barefoot) and ended my day right there.

Perhaps tomorrow will be a better day. Perhaps tomorrow I'll get a new pair of shoes. Because, let me just say, pounding the pavement barefoot is a horribly painful process.

From: **http://www.joseph_stalin.ru/blog/**

Subject: **The Great Purge**

In response to the inordinate amount of notes I've received—yes, I have deleted every single link to every single blog from this site.

It was a purge that was necessary, cleaning house and removing the clutter that suffocated me each and every time I glanced at the site. By getting rid of these blogs (which were, I admit, quite helpful in linking to me in this site's infancy and granting me a great deal of traffic and support), I can now move onward and upward without the deadweight.

In addition, you may or may not have heard that I am enacting laws that will require all Russian bloggers to abandon their personal blogs and begin writing daily for Soviet.com—the daily news, review, culture, art and entertainment portal that the government has been working on for months now. If you are a blogger and you currently have a personal blog, please be aware that such personal blogs will be shut down by the end of the month. Instead, you will be provided a brand-new username and password and required to produce a certain amount of content on a daily basis. I believe that such steps will allow the Russian blogosphere to thrive and grow from this day forth.

Those who are not in agreement with such a change will have their internet connection killed, their accounts suspended, and they will be, for all intents and purposes—"dead to the digital world." I suspect the alternative is better than the punishment.

As part of the premiere of the new Soviet.com collective blog, I would like to direct you to just some of the wonderful pieces that are already available for your perusal:

• Russian Art, How Good It Is

• Stalin, the Extraordinarily Great Person

• My Farm, Your Farm . . . Our Farm

• Stalin, the Extraordinarily Great Person, Pt 2

• Poles and Kalmyks and Chechens, Oh My!

From: **http://www.almighty.com/~adam/**

Subject: **Women!**

Today was not a good day.

Before today, everything was going swimmingly. The lands were bountiful, filled with fruit and food and animals (which I got to name myself, btw) and populated by the lovely Eve. We'd been having some great times, just hanging out and talking until the wee hours of the morning. Seriously, we were in heaven.

Then the you-know-what hit the you-know-what.

Like I've said <u>before</u>, Eve has this thing about not listening to me or the Almighty. The guy tells us we can do whatever we want, whenever we want—full carte blanche. We just can't touch the tree of Knowledge of Good and Evil. That's it. One tree. One little tiny tree that is off limits.

Eve doesn't like things being off limits. If it's something she can't have, you'd better believe she's going to want it. Remember <u>that day</u> she wanted that fig and I had the last fig from the tree? And she threw that temper tantrum for the fig? Perfect example of her having to have exactly what she can't have. (<u>Picture of Eve, eating my fig</u>.)

So I'm out walking around the back of our property today and I turn the corner past the giraffes and the hippos and I see Eve standing there under the tree. What does she have in her hand? An apple. What's missing from that apple? A bite.

"The most delicious apple ever," she says.

Then blah blah blah, she's going on about how *"see, nothing happened"* and how *"it's so good, Adam, just try it"* and *"since I had a bite you should totally try it too or are you not really, truly a man"* kind of thing and she's batting her eyes at me and she's, you know, all there to see.

Women.

About five seconds after taking a taste there's this booming from the sky, the clouds rush in, and you-know-who catches us in the act.

I don't know when I'll be able to write next—we're sort of living in a world of pain now, if you know what I mean.

From: **http://www.brigham_young.com/blog/**

Subject: **Oops!**

Mother's Day is next Sunday.

I don't know, people—what's a guy supposed to get for his wife? You don't want to ask them what they want because, well, that would totally ruin the surprise—but you don't want to just go get them something and then watch them open the gift and realize that no, they don't want an apron. (Yes, I did this last year and was not pleased with the result!)

I know that I'll probably send flowers to <u>Miriam</u>, because she loves daisies and roses. I'll probably get <u>Mary</u> that new iron she was eyeing last week at the store. But what about <u>Lucy</u>? She's so tough to buy for. She says she doesn't want anything but you know that if I don't get her anything, I'll never hear the end of it. Then there's <u>Harriet</u> and <u>Clarissa</u> and the other <u>Clarissa</u>. They want clothing, but I have no idea what size clothing they wear and if I go and ask them what size they are, they're going to know I'm getting them clothing and what kind of surprise is that?

<u>Louisa</u> and <u>Zina</u> and <u>Emily</u> and <u>Eliza</u> and <u>Elizabeth</u> and <u>Diana</u> and <u>Maria</u> and <u>Susannah</u> and <u>Olive</u> and <u>Mary</u> and <u>Margrette</u> are way tough to buy for. They're always finding fault in presents—which doesn't make it much fun to buy them things. But here's a question—sure, I have thirteen kids from these eleven women, but some have never given me a child. Perhaps, possibly, I don't have to get them a present? Or a less expensive one? Right, men? <u>Chime in</u>.

Thing is, last year I didn't get presents for some of my wives who have never had children (<u>Rhoda</u>, <u>Mary</u>, <u>Mary Ann</u>, <u>Emily</u>, <u>Abigail</u>, <u>Mary E.</u> and <u>Amy C.</u> immediately come to mind) and they totally felt out of place while <u>Emmeline</u>, <u>Margaret Maria</u>, <u>Lucy</u> and <u>Harriet</u> opened their gifts. Boy was that a rough night. You know who had to spend the night with the OTHER forty-three wives after being kicked to the curb by the first seven? Yes, you guessed it. Ol' Brigham Young was getting the classic cold shoulder.

Maybe tonight I'll try to casually guess what <u>Hannah</u>, <u>Lydia</u>, <u>Elizabeth J.</u>, <u>Ann Eliza</u>, <u>Mary C.</u> and <u>Mary O.</u> might want. I've got ten minutes with each of them tonight, so that should be just enough time to figure out what's on their "extra special gift lists" this time of year! Maybe I'll just ask. Oh, who knows!

It's just so darn hard trying to buy for Mother's Day.

If all else fails, I guess I can ask the kids. Between fifty-six of them, someone's bound to come up with an idea, right?

Gosh, I hope so.

From: **http://www.homer.gr/blog/**
Subject: **Where Are Thou, O Muse?**

Here I sit, in silence, staring up at this stone—draped in white, without any words.

The words, so quickly they came to my head and my hand before—the *Iliad* the result of such vivid apparitions. The siege on Ilium and the Trojan War played out in my mind, and in the minds of those who sat to hear the tale. O Muse, how we knew each other so well during those times, and all men they did rally behind the tale, speaking the words to others and those to others again. The *Iliad*, a success, had become.

And now, with the pressure upon me, I cannot find the words for the second tale.

O Muse, where are thou? A title, you have not given me—although a story of an odyssey I suspect might be nice. The story of Odysseus, King of Ithaca, after the war which raged upon Troy. But what of his actions? His adventures to come? The influence of the gods? My mind is a blank, and there is nothing for me to tell.

I am at a loss for words, O Muse, and the people they grow more impatient by the day. Where is thou Odyssey they pose. When shall we hear the tale they say. Why has there not been a second story with so much time passing since the first?

Perhaps, O Muse, one is all there ever was inside of me? So says me, writer and poet. One perhaps is all there is. For what else explanation can there be for a man so prolific yet so completely absent of ideas?

For who can fault a man for writing once with greatness and allowing that to mark him for life? No man can fault another for such. But when greatness falls, replaced by mediocrity (with another story that does not inspire)—then the mark darkens, and failure overshadows.

Perhaps this odyssey will never occur. Perhaps Odysseus' journey ends in the *Iliad*. Perhaps my Muse has decided for me—that a second project is not my destiny.

But that must not be true. Yet I have nothing to give. But the first, such a rousing success. Where are my thoughts? Why to me, does this occur?

I have nothing to give. I cannot. No. I cannot. I cannot.

But they ask for more. And more. And more!

A meal. Perhaps a meal will help spark the hidden tale of Odysseus. Entertainment of some kind. A meal and entertainment and a well-needed break. Yes! This is my destiny.

When I have returned, then I shall try again.

From: **http://www.pope_john_paul_II.it/papal-blog/**
Subject: **The Raddest Day Ever**

Are you ready for this!? Totally crazy. Seriously. Out of control.

So I'm sleeping in my quarters, right? It's like five in the morning or something, pretty early, tryin' to get my rest after a night of blessing a bunch of people here at the Vatican. Anyway—I open my eyes for a split second to flip over and get to the cold side of the bed when I spot like twenty cardinals . . . get this . . . Wait for it . . . IN MY ROOM!

I almost freaked out! I mean, usually we'll all meet up downstairs but never have they all come like that and stood so freakishly quiet in the corner of my room. I was like, *"Yo, what's going on, Cardinals?"* and they were like, *"Holy Father . . . we have some-thing to show you that you might want to see"* and blah blah blah blah blah . . . More of that for a while and I was like, *"Well, you woke me up already, I ain't goin' back to sleep so let's go see what you have to show me."*

So I get on a robe and shorts and I'm following the cardinals downstairs, and yeah my stomach is rumbling and stuff (I had like nothing to eat the night before, I totally spaced) and they gently urge me to walk into the courtyard and you . . . will . . . not . . . believe . . . what was there.

The most raddest, most awesomest, most amazing thing ever. A brand-new car, with a huge red ribbon around it. The cardinals hand me the keys. It was crazy!

I'm like, *"You guys got me a brand-new Pope Mobile!"* I'm shaking and stuff, running around this bulletproof beauty. I mean, this thing is sweet. And then one of the cardi-nals leans in and he's like, *"It's a modified Range Rover, Holy Father . . ."*

Okay. If you could have seen my eyes right then you would have FREAKED OUT. A Range Rover? A Range Rover. So not only is this baby bulletproof and I can stand up in this thing and wave to everyone and if someone shoots at me there's no way that bullet's gonna touch my skin like last time . . . But it's also a Range Rover. It's like, too cool. Functional, secure, and a pretty nice car. And you know what else? The Vatican pays for the insurance. And the gas. I felt like I was on *The Price Is Right*—here I am, in my bathrobe staring at my brand-new ride.

So I get inside and start this baby up and I'm doing 360s around the courtyard there and the cardinals are lookin' on and stuff and I'm just peeling out. It was really the most awesome present ever, and I can't wait to do some exploring in it later today.

'Course, they keep wanting to call this thing the "Papal Limousine" but I put down my foot and told these guys it has to be called the Pope Mobile. That's just a sweet, hip name for it. None of this stuffy, Papal Limousine stuff. Pope Mobile.

Yeaaaah. You gotta love it!

From: **http://www.nixon.com/checkersblog/**

My fellow Americans—my inbox has been overwhelmed with correspondence since last week's appearance on national TV. Pat, Tricia, Julie, and I are so thankful that you embraced our adorable little black and white spotted cocker spaniel dog—who we call Checkers.

The above picture is me and Checkers just outside on the White House lawn. Checkers was absolutely tired after a day of fetch and playing ball. If you'd like to see Checkers jumping up on his hind legs and walking on two feet, click here.

Little Jason Babsiewski (jbabsiew@aol.com) from Olympia, Washington, sent this amazing artistic re-creation of Checkers to me the other day. I think you'll agree that it's quite a resemblance! Checkers looks just as regal and thoughtful as he does when he's sitting next to me on the carpet in the Oval Office.

Remember when I mentioned about the man in Texas who heard Pat on the radio when she said that our daughters would like to have a dog? Well, I must tell you that the crate he sent Checkers in to us was well padded and comfortable for the little guy. Here's a picture of him at ten months old.

Checkers
10 mos old

There are even <u>more pictures</u> for your viewing pleasure of Checkers eating, playing, sleeping and <u>chewing his favorite toy</u>.

I will say it again—no matter what people say, we are keeping Checkers. He is a wonderful new addition to the family and my daughters would absolutely be heartbroken without him. Pat loves him too.

CHECKERS'S DAILY UPDATE:
Checkers went for three walks today with his official White House dog walker. He went pee three times, making sure to mark his territory, then went poop once by the back veranda behind the Oval Office and on the hallway carpet in the family wing of the White House. There was a moment when one of my aides had to grab a piece of you-know-what that was hanging by a single strand of hair and Checkers was extremely confused. But he was calm, cool and collected and all ended up perfect in the end! Good job, Checkers!

LINKS:

<u>AKC Cocker Spaniel Information</u>

<u>My Cocker Spaniel, Toopsey</u> (Our friends')

<u>Cocker Spaniel Tips and Training</u>

<u>Cocker Spaniel Sweaters & Hoodies</u>

<u>My Doggy, Checkers—Essay by Tricia Nixon</u>

From: **http://www.rembrandt.com/blog/**
Subject: **My Stalker, Helmut, Returns . . .**

Perhaps it may be time to refrain from publishing this blog.

Saskia and I moved into the Jodenbreestraat in the Jewish Quarter to get away from the chaos that had followed us previously. You may recall the entry about my fan, Helmut, who sent me over 100 messages in one day in an attempt to gain my attention, as he was "my most dedicated and supportive fan."

You may also remember how I disregarded such messages as I was advised to, not knowing the seriousness of the situation and preferring to leave well enough alone. When I found Helmut in our downstairs crawlspace under the stairs (where he had been living for thirteen days without food or water) we decided the move (which we had previously talked about doing) was the smartest thing to do.

The last few days have been less than tranquil.

Even without listing our new address or contact information, Helmut has found us again. Three days ago Saskia and I awoke to find Helmut sitting at the edge of our bed, dressed in a full coat of armor—looking exactly like a figure I painted in *The Blinding of Sampson*. Saskia and I stared blankly as he rattled off my entire body of work, asking questions as to why I used this color or what the allegory of certain pieces related to or if he could live with us forever. I cautiously told Helmut that this harassment must stop.

Helmet was noticeably upset, resulting in him ripping apart various portions of the room while Saskia slipped out to call for help. Eventually, local authorities carted him away (again), resulting in another statement being given by yours truly.

It seems that we will have to stand against Helmut in a court, in an attempt to legally force him to stay away from our new home. It seems Helmut was able to track our location from certain payment slips used by me to fund this online service.

Thus is the reason for my possible decision in removing this site from the public eye. I have had no luck getting any new pieces done since this harassment has begun, and I choose to nip it as quickly as I can.

I will, however, keep you up to date on the current case against this man.

Questions or comments to Rembrandt@amsterdamonline.com.

From: **http://www.ansel_adams.com/photoblog/**

Subject: **School's Out . . . Forever!**

Mother and Father let me quit school last week.

The other thirteen-year-olds were so jealous that I don't have to go anymore, that I can just learn what I want to learn at home with my parents. <u>Frederick</u> says that if you don't go to school you'll never succeed in life, but I don't care what he has to say about that. I never liked going there, and whether or not it was because I was bored or because people made fun of the fact that I was color-blind . . . Well, I don't care!

Now I can concentrate on learning and practicing piano. Mother has arranged for my lessons to continue and my hope is that I may someday be a well-regarded pianist who can travel the landscapes of the world—bringing music everywhere.

It is a little boring around the house with no one but adults to talk to.

I told mother that I wished there was something else I could do besides practice and study and she responded by giving me a gift—a photographic camera. A camera. How can a color-blind person use a camera?

Mother said that I didn't have to always tell people I was color-blind—it could be a secret among the close family. That people didn't have to know. That just because I couldn't see colors didn't mean that I couldn't use a camera. I told her I wanted to play piano instead and so she put away the camera and didn't mention another thing about it.

In a few months, the family will be going to Yosemite National Park—we're going camping! That helps to think about when I'm sitting here at home trying to study and trying to practice. That will be so much fun.

From: **http://www.winston_churchill.co.uk/speech-blog/**

Subject: **Never Give In . . . Never Give Up . . .**

"Never give in. Never give in. Never, never, never, never—in nothing, great or small, large or petty—never give in . . ."

Do you know which soldier and journalist spoke those words? Do you know who wrote that speech? Would you be surprised to know that it was ME? Sir Winston Churchill? Yes. It was ME. I wouldn't kid with you. On my honor. These words are mine!

"We shall fight on the beaches. We shall fight on the landing grounds. We shall fight in the fields and in the streets, we shall fight in the hills. We shall never surrender!"

Do you know which author and politician spoke those words and WROTE that speech? Would you be surprised that, once again, such superior oratory skills can be directly linked to ME? Sir Winston Churchill? You're saying to yourself right now, "I can't believe Sir Winston Churchill is so astute, intelligent, and inspiring!"

But I am.

Would you be surprised to know that you, too, can benefit from my well-respected, well-regarded, well-honed speechwriting skills and know-how?

From weddings to funerals to college graduation ceremonies, <u>Churchill Speaks</u> is a new service I am launching today that will craft unique and personal prose for you, the not-so-good-at-writing-speeches individual. And for a competitively low price, we will craft, perfect and deliver to you on note cards (included in the price) the kind of speech people will be talking about for years after. Just read what some of our satisfied customers are already saying:

<u>Jimmy12</u> writes, *"My grandfather had just passed away and his last wish was that I speak at his funeral. I was terrified to stand up in front of such a large group and had nothing to say. Thanks to Churchill Speaks, my speech about Granddad and never giving up and never giving in, sure inspired the crowd—although some had no idea what my speech had to do with Granddad . . . But who cares! It was an inspiring moment they'll never forget!"*

Anonymous31 writes, "*I didn't have time to study for my oral history report on the U.S. government's Depiction of War to the Public in the First World War, but thanks to Churchill Speaks I gave a rousing speech about fighting in the streets and in the fields and above all . . . never surrendering! And although it didn't even make sense, I still got an A thanks to Churchill's amazingly well-written words!*"

Jim211@srn.net writes, "*After losing a local mayoral election, I needed a speech that could communicate the fact that I would be stepping down from the post. Although the speech I got from Churchill Speaks was about not giving up or surrendering . . . I still felt pretty good up there giving the speech to my, um, wife.*"

Are you someone who is afraid to speak? Afraid that your words just won't impress? Want to make sure that while you're up in front of others, that it is your **"finest hour"**? Then take it from me, Sir Winston Churchill—my words sound amazing coming out of anyone's mouth. So why not make it YOU?

'Twas early this morning of Christmas Eve that I awoke with a start, enveloped in the darkness—my brow wet with worry and my thoughts filled with fear.

While sound asleep, of which I was, visions of my daily work filled my head. The words of which I slave over, hour to hour and day to day, on the pages of the physical world and on this ghostly screen at which you stare this very moment.

This weblog, which I endeavour to fill without fail each and every day, has undoubtedly become a true test of wills—at times requiring the posts of future days to be written ahead of time so that my dear readers are never left without a tale. On this early morning of Christmas Eve, my inner specters came calling to test my righteousness and dedication of this cause.

In my dreams, an aged spirit appeared at first, pulling at my arm and showing me that which has passed me by—the past blog entries which I've penned. Not particularly fearful was I, yet the perfectionist inside of me grew critical by the moment at the lack of professionalism associated with such writings. Colourful as they were, there was an amateurish nature at their core—the spirit of blogs past written suggested that in order to succeed I must never return to such simplemindedness. My writings of the past were not thoughtful, rather, they were extremely innocent and perhaps slightly mean-spirited . . .

The beat of my heart moved along at a normal pace throughout it all, as the friendly spirits seemed to be there to help. And where one had appeared, another took its place—this time a friendly spirit who showed me my present ramblings. This spirit of the present revealed an image of myself, rushing to finish my daily entries—shortcuts abound. While the quality had improved tenfold, the heart was no longer there. "Empty words, posted daily," the spirit spoke. It was no way of sending goodwill to those in need of inspiring words or heartfelt tales. As soon as the vision appeared, it was gone.

The chime struck three as I awoke on my knees, looking up to a figure that was no longer there. Doubt in my head, I wandered back to the warmth of my bed—at least confident that what I had written and scheduled to appear almost magically on the following day (due to my lack of time on the morrow) would impress and inspire. Yet as soon as I found myself drifting—a third creature appeared. More horrible than the last two combined, this spirit showed me the most spine-tingling future existence.

An existence where that which I had postdated for the future had never appeared whatsoever. The words I had planned for the future's consideration sat stoic in a menu system, waiting to appear but never choosing to do so.

"Is this the future of my blog entry?" I wondered aloud to the spirit.

The wisest of all three, it nodded and I awoke with a start—was everything I had seen simply a vision or was there truth to this horrible future? I raced to my devices, turned them on, and looked into the future of my entries.

And there, as I had dreamed, it stood outright—morrow's post dated for a year ahead instead of a mere hours away. The hairs on the back of my neck stood straight—the visits I had encountered throughout the night had appeared to teach a lesson outright. A lesson, of which I would never forget . . . I would never again write for the future, hoping it would appear magically to my readers. Instead, I would not take the shortcut, and I would write for the day, on the day—and be a better man because of it.

Never again would I utter "Aaah, dumb-blog!" out of frustration or a lack of respect for this wondrous place.

Never again.

From: **http://www.abner_doubleday.com/blog/**

Subject: **Uh, Baseball?**

Is it just me, or is baseball completely, utterly <u>boring</u>!?

I made it out for the National League World Series last week in Chicago (yes, the Chicago White Stockings won it!) and can I just say this without anyone gettin' all up in my face or anything . . . But, man—whoever invented the damn game should've at least tried to make it ENTERTAINING to watch!!

Can I just say that I would rather get shot in the neck with a bullet (and I was, during the Battle of Gettysburg) than sit through an entire game of this booooooooring spectator sport? You got guys standing out in the field, waiting. You got guys standing in the infield, waiting. You got a guy with a bat on the home plate, waiting. Everyone's waiting for a ball to get hit and so is the crowd. And in the meantime? You wait. Then something happens, and it's over in a second, and you go back to waiting. I could go sit in the doctor's office and wait for an appointment and have more fun.

You'd think they'd have some good food there or something, but that's missing too.

Yeah, yeah—take it up with the guys who invented the damn game. I only wish that I could. You know, I'd have to head back to England for that with them and their games of cricket and rounders . . . Doesn't it all make sense anyway? The English are boring and reserved and quiet. What do you expect from a game whose origins come from their own country?

Yawn.

When I was a kid, back in New York, sure we used to play around with the ball and run around out there in the field but it was fun because we could make up our own rules. I especially liked the game that I came up with called "Throw It and Catch It." That's where someone would throw the ball and someone else would catch it. Man, we played that for hours and it never got boring because you were always doing something. But baseball—yeah, we never played much of that. Prolly 'cause we didn't ever have enough people and because, and I say this with all the respect in the world . . . it was the most BORING game ever.

Doubt I'll ever make it back to another game, if only 'cause I just don't have the time to waste. Sure, if I invented the damn game or owned one of the teams then maybe I'd feel more invested in the game. But until that day, well, I ain't stepping one foot into a baseball park again.

At least, not until they get some good food.

From: **http://www.gandhi.org/moblog/**

Subject: **From the Front Lines of Oppression**

With so much to accomplish, I have taken to the streets in an attempt to communicate with all of you via my mobile device. As you very well know, I have now been fasting for twenty days to oppose the British oppression here in India.

Mmmm, someone just walked by with a hot dog.

But, alas—I will continue what they call this "civil disobedience" in lieu of the violence they expect. I object to violence because when it appears to do good, the good is only temporary; the evil it does is permanent. This, I stand behind—these words that I have bread.

Er, said. These words that I have **said**. Not bread. There was a nice young woman standing next to me as I typed that selection of words. She was holding a hot, steaming, mouthwatering, soft and lovely, joyful loaf of bread. But she has gone now. And all is food. Er, **good**. All is **good**.

Some of you have expressed your beliefs that such actions are without merit. Yet, are our minds this much like Swiss cheese, do the holes in our memory cause us to forget the Dandi March of 1930? An act of such civil disobedience that it resulted in a signed pact between the British one year later—do we forget so fast?

Yes, such false promises regarding setting political prisoners free came and went without any resolution, and after talks fell through—this latest fast was necessary. And so here I sit, twenty days without any food—protesting the British for their treatment of our people. For their lack of respect, understanding and inability to drink . . .

Er, **think**.

I, er, have a few things to take care of, but will post more at a later lime . . . er **time**.

From: **http://www.benito_mussolini.it/blog/**

Subject: **Il Duce Blogger!**

If you are reading these words, as written by Il Duce Blogger, you have no further need for any other blog-ger you have previously read. Now is the time to throw away your bookmarks and abandon your feeds, as Il Duce Blogger can provide you with everything you could possibly need here in the blogosphere.

The Italian press has recently printed a variety of articles on Il Duce Blogger (here, here, here, here and here) and has said . . .

> *" . . . Il Duce Blogger never sleeps!"*

> *" . . . Il Duce Blogger is always right!"*

> *"He will solve all the problems of the blogosphere!"*

As Il Duce Blogger (your leader in blogging), my goal will be to provide for you, the worker with too much time on their hands during the daylight hours, an outlet for your spare moments . . . A place to read about what should be important to you in your lives . . . A place where I will tell you what everyone thinks is important, at which point you too will agree that these are the things you should be concentrating on.

> *"Everyone reads Il Duce Blogger, even children!"*

It seems that such is true—even children who have yet to fully be capable of reading entire sen-tences are reading the words of yours truly, Il Duce Blogger. And why not? Teachers throughout all of Italy have decided that old textbooks are simply outdated and useless. Instead, they have turned to this blog—introducing and supporting Il Duce Blogger!

And in a surprise to even yours truly, it seems as though every aspect of the press has voluntarily jumped onboard the Il Duce Blogger wagon! Newspapers, books, radio, film—they are all in sup-port of Il Duce Blogger!

On a not so positive note, it seems that those who have yet to embrace the writings of Il Duce Blogger are being dragged into the streets and attacked by my true blog supporters. This is, of course, not something I endorse and I hope that those who fall into this category will simply change their alliances and delete old bookmarks before those close to them realize where their allegiance lies.

The answers to every single one of your questions await!

From: **http://www.bruce_lee.ch/blog/** *

*(Disclaimer: Bruce Lee's Chinese-language blog has been translated into English for his North American fans using an online translation service that may or may not change the meanings of a few isolated words.)

Subject: **Lives in Automobile Trumpet Kong!**

I write to you from mine family in Hong Kong.

My here comes at first with Linda therefore we can attend *Big Boss Shield*. Some many people in theater. All is extremely excitedly looked the movie and it is even more exciting causes me to meet my zealous frantic amateur.

It is different here in Hong Kong.

I felt like I am respected replace in mine motherland I to treat in US'S way. This feels. From then on, the movie has been distributed, I accept many propositions to hold the post of the lead in other movies.

I receive a telegram to inform me from Los Angeles, I not to obtain the work today to say "in them; Soldier name television program." They, instead, employ a Caucasian to play Kung the Fu master, I discovered extremely insults. This is the reason I decided pauses and obtains the work in Hong Kong at other movies. I have control here to the product, respects me with this country the work.

I and start with Linda to converse about possibly open martial arts center here in Hong Kong. I have been able to teach the fist way which intercepts and other people to be able to profit from any me for many years the academic society. I am firmly these practices wing spring Gung the Fu technology may not seek pleasure by this decision, but is I thought this is best for me.

I must thank my supporters in there for me. My ventilators! You, I could not be I am today place. Your support is the nonprice. Your note is appreciated. My ventilators! Without you I one all day have not been able to sleep. Without you I have not been able to give wearily. But instead, not. My ventilators are the reason.

If you come and you reads my word from US, thanks visits this place!

If you meet want to converse with me, send to me to write down <u>here</u>.

From: **http://www.king_arthur.uk/blog/**

Subject: **Meeting Bloggers for the First Time!**

Dare I say I was quite nervous just a fortnight ago? Would that strike you as being strange for me, King Arthur?

Perhaps, but I must be honourable and be honest when I write that my nerves were not that of steel, were not as strong as my shield or my sword . . . My knees, nervous with worry, for whatever silly reason—I simply hoped that the others I was about to meet would find me as interesting in person as they had found me here . . . on this blog.

You've seen their names here before in the feedback section. Bloggers who are knights and knights who are bloggers—courageously fighting evil and bad sentence structure all at once. We had agreed eons ago to sit down together, in person—and this moment was a long time coming.

Of course, when I entered the room I found myself having trouble with the words, but eventually they came out perfectly. <u>Sir Galahad</u> approached first, handing me a stein of the finest ale around. His nerves were shot as well—which he admitted as we moved to the center table where we met <u>Sir Gareth</u> and <u>Sir Aglovale</u> (son of King Pellinore), <u>Sir Florence</u> and <u>Sir Bors</u>. And of course, who could not forget the confident and personable <u>Sir Lancelot</u>? Not I. That 'tis for sure.

'Twas a good showing with almost twenty or more of our blogger-knights, and after hours had passed and good words were exchanged, the lot of us all looked up from the table at which we sat and it hit us. I believe it was <u>Sir Tristam</u> who said, *"Here we sit, knights at this round table, bloggers first in heart, knights second in courage. This table is awfully nice as well, whose is it? I particularly like the roundness of it . . ."*

Well, the table was owned by the establishment, of course—but Tristam's thoughts were well received. It was then, at that moment, we all came to agreement on our official formation of an organization whose ultimate goal above all would be to meet regularly for a bloggers roundtable. Writing, form, subject matter and grammatical issues plaguing the bloggers across these great lands. The moment of our formation would never be forgotten.

All in all, a very exciting time for the kingdom and I'm glad to say that I was honored to meet each and every one of my new brothers, and even more pleased that I made it throughout the night without losing my dinner all over the floor.

External Link: <u>Royal Bloggers Website</u>

From: # http://www.philistine.g0Liath.com/blog/
Subject: # Israelite.c0m Hack3d!

I am th3 uLtiM4t3. (Click <u>h3re</u> for the cha0s.)

Check 0ut Israelite.c0m and t3LL me that isn't the m0st hilari0us thing you've ever s33n. It t00k me 40 days to do it, but my sup3ri0r hacK1ng skiLLz triumph3d and they'LL nev3R get the uLtiM4t3 . . . g0Liath.

I am t00 g00d f0r th0se small mind3d, puny Israelites!

Posted by g0Liath at 6:11 AM | Permalink | Comments (7)

C0MM3NTS

You're not THAT good. We've tracked your domain name to an address in the Valley of Elah. I'm going to take you down.

Posted by: David | 6:15 AM

What3ver. Y0u d0nt sc4re me, runt.

Posted by: G0Liath | 6:28 AM

Not only do we know you're in the Valley of Elah, but we know you're from Gath. You've got family there, don't you? I'm sure they'd love to know what barbaric things you're doing to other people's sites.

Posted by: David | 7:01 AM

Big wh00p. Any0n3 wiTh half a bra1n c0uLd figur3 that 0ut.

Posted by: G0Liath | 8:21 AM

We're gonna cut the snake off at the head, if you know what I mean.

Posted by: David | 9:23 AM

So c0m3 aNd get m3, c0w4rd!

Posted by: G0Liath | 9:41 AM

Look out your tent. You should see me standing about 100 feet from your camp on the mountain.

Posted by: David | 9:49 AM

COMMENTS CLOSED BY HOST

From: **http://www.benfranklin.org/blog/**

Subject: **Journaling June, Seventeen Hundred Fifty-two**

I so blacked out again last night.

So get this—I totally wake up this morning, way wiped, facedown in what tastes like a puddle of rainwater, a bunch of street kids dancing around me like I was some kind of fat pig at a picnic. I am OUT OF IT. There's some damn cloth and string tied up all around me and a big ol' key in my hands. I bolted as quick as I could get myself untangled—I didn't need the attention.

Look, at least it wasn't as bad as <u>last time</u>, when I woke up after those bastard Founding Fathers wrote less than cool nicknames all over my forehead in black ink. And it wasn't nearly as embarrassing as the time I found myself stark naked and wrapped in a half-finished American flag. Doh! A certain BR was none too pleased that I had soiled her hard work.

But what is UP with this whole cloth string key thing? I don't know if any of you saw me out partying it up last night but if you did and you can tell me what the hell I ended up doing last night, do me a big one and <u>e-mail me</u>. Seriously. Man, my head is friggin' throbbing right now. Oh, and get this! I totally just realized that someone shaved or burnt my eyebrows off! I got black soot marks all over my damn body.

I'll bet you it was Adams. That guy is always talkin' about shaving people's eyebrows off and lighting them on fire. Come to think of it, Adams was also the guy who spearheaded the whole "write on Franklin's forehead with ink while he's passed out" thing. He's always drunk, that's probably why. Man, what is this key for?

Anyway—to recap: I am clueless as to last night's events. Give me a holler if you got anything to share.

From: **http://www.jack_ruby.com/blog/**
Subject: **Liveblogging JFK's Assassination!**

Nov 22, 12:30pm: President Kennedy has been shot. No, I am NOT JOKING. Turn on your radio. I was just watching it on TV and I couldn't believe my eyes. OK. Okay. I'm, I just don't know what I can tell you . . . I am SO ANGRY.

12:32pm: Still VERY angry. Kennedy is en route to a hospital. There's no way he's going to survive that shot. I can tell. Who did it? No idea. Some Commie bastard, I'm sure of it.

12:33pm: Just kicked in part of the wall in the bathroom. Made me feel a little bit better.

12:34pm: Angry again.

12:38pm: Kennedy just arrived at Parkland Hospital. I hope they have good doctors there. I've never been to the Parkland Hospital but I gotta tell ya—I would never go to a hospital that had the word "park" in its name. That's like going to a hospital where the word "fun" is in its name. Someplace called Funland Hospital. There's no serious medicine being practiced there, I can tell you that GODDAMMIT.

12:40pm: TV isn't working anymore. Had to switch to radio. Antenna on the TV has been on the fritz lately. Waiting to hear if they caught anyone. Keep you up to date.

12:43pm: Okay. I kicked in the TV. I didn't want to mention that above, but I was angry. This is CRAZY. I am SO MAD.

12:45pm: Police are getting somewhere. Suspect is slender white male about thirty, five feet ten, one sixty-five, carrying what looked to be a 30.30 or some type of Winchester. Says he was in the Book Depository. Locking it down.

12:53pm: Seeing red. Blowing in paper bag. So very angry. Sad, too. More angry then sad. A sad/angry combination. About 30% sad, 70% angry.

12:57pm: Update on anger percentage: 10% sad, 90% angry.

1:00pm: Kennedy declared dead. 100% angry.

[Update: Suspect in custody. Something Oswald.]

[Update 2: I can't do this anymore. 120% angry, −20% sad. I have things to take care of. I'll be back. No blogging for the next few days. Gonna take a break.]

Angryangryangry.

From: **http://www.marquis_de_sade.fr/blog/**

Subject: **An Apology to Renee**

Baby doll. Darlin'. I'm sorry. No, not sorry like last time—REALLY sorry.

Darlin', I hope you are reading these words and you can hear the disappointment in them. The disappointment in myself. I know that I am not the man you expected me to be and I apologize for hurting you in any way. The first few times when I hurt you, you said nothing—you simply skulked away and remained silent. How was I to know that you felt as if I had crossed a line in our marriage? I never meant to hurt you. I do have control over myself, unlike what you have vocalized to me, and these horrible painful things that I have done to you, I . . . They fill my . . . Just thinking about them makes me . . . I . . .

Sorry, I am back. There was someone at the door.

As I was saying, my little love-muffin—I never meant to hurt you. I know you believe me when I tell you that you mean more to me than anything, and if I ever put you in a position where you felt like I was harming you, it was simply an accident that . . . I . . . Uh, oooh yeah . . .

Had to get a glass of water . . . Anyway—

You gotta forgive me, baby. Accept my apology for these things which you find abhorrent. I am a good man. You make me want to be a better man. Having the police come to our door that night after I supposedly "abused" you was not the right thing to do, if I may say so myself. Bringing strangers from the outside into our lives adds complication to an already complicated relationship. You must know, deep down, that when I whip you it means I care for you more than I can express in words . . . You should know, that when I strap you into those painful contraptions, that it means I long for us to grow old together . . .

This is why I wanted to apologize to you here, for all the world to see. So you knew, that I had grown, that I had matured, and that I can put these painful hobbies behind m—

Sorry, I'm back. Where was I? Oh—I apologize.

Please forgive me, darling. It will never happen again!

[Webmaster note: Looking for <u>pictures</u> and <u>erotic stories</u>? Click to read.]

From: **http://www.c.s.lewis.com/blog/**

Subject: **Mother's Story**

"There's a lying witch in the wardrobe," she said. *"She sleeps there, waiting for curious children who enjoy playing with their mother's bras to come calling. And then, as they're about to put her expensive bras on their head and play knights and dragons, well, the witch will awaken and strike them dead right on the spot!!"*

Mother told Warren and me that story for years following the "bra incident of 1907" in which expensive bras became expensive warrior headdresses and armbands, painted in the colours of our tribes. As I got older, and smarter, I still feared this "lying witch."

Then I got to thinking. If she was a "lying witch" she should be telling untruths. If she was sleeping in there, she should be "a witch lying down in the wardrobe." It was about then that her entire story unraveled and I realized that the grammatical inconsistencies pointed to the falsehoods being spun by mother dearest.

Still there was always something catchy about there being a "lying witch in the wardrobe." I guess you could say, it's a phrase that's always been with me. Sooner or later, I'll find a way to scare other small children with just that.

I shared the story with my fellow <u>Inklings</u> here at Oxford (the literary discussion group I frequent) and friend <u>J.R.R.</u> suggested turning such a short story into an elaborate tale of hidden worlds and beloved objects. I suggested that a missing bra from my mother could not be the cause of adventure and conflict, and that's when he suggested perhaps that I make it a bracelet or ring of my mother's that had gone missing—that which all creatures in this world were after. Nothing rang true, it seemed, but it was a lively discussion nonetheless.

"There's a lying witch in the wardrobe . . ."

Indeed. Indeed there is.

From: **http://www.b_f_skinner.com/skinner-blog/**

Subject: **Experiment #45D (No Instructions Available)**

CLICK ON THIS BUTTON TO READ AN ENTRY ON **MY WEEKEND.**

ARE YOU INTERESTED IN A SKINNER-BLOG T-SHIRT? CLICK THIS BUTTON AND YOU MAY VERY WELL BE REWARDED WITH ONE.

ARE YOU HUNGRY?

BY CLICKING ON THIS BUTTON YOU WILL BE GIVEN A POLL THAT YOU MUST ANSWER HONESTLY. IF YOU DO NOT ANSWER HONESTLY YOU WILL NEVER BE GIVEN THE CHANCE TO CLICK ANOTHER BUTTON.

THIS BUTTON IS BLACK. CLICK IF YOU LOVE BLACK.

IF YOU WOULD LIKE TO BE ADDED AS A LINK ON THIS BLOG, CLICK ON THIS BUTTON, THEN CLICK ON ALL THE OTHER BUTTONS, AND REPEAT EVERY DAY FOR SEVEN (7) CONSECUTIVE DAYS.

CLICKING REPEATEDLY ON THIS BUTTON WILL DO YOU NO GOOD, AS IT IS BROKEN. THIS LINK IS BROKEN. DO NOT CLICK ON IT. I REPEAT, THIS BUTTON IS BROKEN, SO THERE IS NO NEED FOR YOU TO BE CLICKING ON IT.

From: **http://www.blognation.ch/~SunTzu/**

Subject: **The Art of Blogging**

Thanks to the success of *The Art of War*, I have decided to turn my attention toward the next frontier that affects the State. The art of blogging. I have spent much time coming up with a wholly original, extremely unique document to address this new-found artistic endeavor. Any similarity to *The Art of War* is purely coincidental.

I will continue to share examples from this upcoming text with you, here, on a daily basis. Your thoughts are welcome.

· The art of blogging is of vital importance to the State.

· All blogging is based on deception.

· Hence, when able to post, we must seem unable; when using our creative thoughts, we must seem uncreative; when we are near to posting, we must make our readers believe we are far from it; when far from posting, we must make our readers believe we are near.

· Now in order to cause your readers to post comments, they must be roused to anger; that there may be advantage from engaging such readers, they must have their rewards (like a free T-shirt or something).

· A distracting background song may weaken your blogging oppo-nents, while a pleasant one may make them stronger; this is why you must choose wisely instead of not choosing at all.

· Your links are only as strong as those who stand behind such links; one weak link will act as a hole in your literary armor.

- While linking to a popular blog entry gives you strength in numbers, writing an original post makes you stronger as one, where many spread over the land to read one post repeated again and again, your followers' numbers will rise when you are the sole author of one post entirely.

- The principle on leaving negative comments is clear, while a man who leaves negative comments is well known for his negativeness, a man who leaves positive comments is barely known at all—this keeps his identity unknown for when anonymity is necessary.

- A blog with an easy-to-remember URL may garner many visitors and positive word of mouth, but it will never gain the respect of a URL that is hard to find; that which people seek out will always gain the most respect.

- If you must destroy a fellow blogger, then you must destroy a fellow blogger.

Other projects that are also currently in progress include <u>The Art of "The Art of War"</u>, <u>More "Art of War"</u>, <u>Some Things You May Not Know About "The Art of War"</u>, <u>"The Art of War: The Beginning"</u> and <u>Hot Steamed Rice in Less Than One Hour</u>.

Index to Bloggers

ABOUT THE AUTHOR

PAUL DAVIDSON is the author of *Consumer Joe: Harassing Corporate America, One Letter at a Time.* In addition to writing for film and TV, he is a regular contributor to *Wired, mental_floss,* NPR, and his own blog, *Words for My Enjoyment* (www.pauldavidson.net). He lives in Los Angeles with his wife and dog, who cares more about liver treats than being included here . . . but what the hell.